FIRE STORM
THE GREAT FIRES OF 1918

Smoldering remains of a rural homestead after the fire of 1918.

Photo by Hugh McKenzie from the collection of CCHS

FIRE STORM
THE GREAT FIRES OF 1918

Christine Skalko
Marlene Wisuri

Carlton County Historical Society
Cloquet, Minnesota

FUNDING SPONSORS

This book is printed on 60# Patina Matte Text and Aero Cover Stock, made possible through a grant to the Carlton County Historical Society from Sappi Fine Papers of Cloquet.

Cloquet Educational Foundation

Edwin F. and Mary Erickson

Lake Country Power

Members Co-operative Credit Union

Thrivent Financial for Lutherans

Wells Fargo Bank, Cloquet

Copyright © 2003 Carlton County Historical Society

All rights reserved. No part of this book may be reproduced in any form, except excerpts for review and for classroom use without the written permission of the publisher.

Carlton County Historical Society
406 Cloquet Avenue
Cloquet, MN 55720
218/879-1938
www.carltoncountyhs.org

Cover photos from the collections of CCHS and MLAHS

Printed and bound in the United States of America
by Bang Printing, Brainerd, Minnesota.
Book layout and design by Marlene Wisuri

ISBN 0-9618959-6-9

Dedicated

to the fire sufferers and their families with the hope that their stories will not be forgotten.

TABLE OF CONTENTS

ABOUT THIS BOOK	**8**
INTRODUCTION	**11**
CHAPTER 1: BEFORE THE FIRE	**15**
Conditions	15
Lack of Fire Safety and Prevention Practices	17
Lack of Fire Fighting Equipment, Supplies, & Trained Firefighters	18
Lack of an Effective Communication System	18
CHAPTER 2: THE CLOQUET FIRE BEGINS	**21**
Milepost 62	21
The Fond du Lac Indian Reservation	23
Rural Areas Are Ablaze	26
CHAPTER 3: THE FIRE ENTERS CLOQUET	**29**
The City Is Alerted to the Approaching Fire	29
The Townspeople Prepare to Leave	30
Escape by Train	30
Escape by Foot	33
Escape by Automobile	33
Fury of the Flames Sweeps City	34
The Harrowing Train Ride	35
The Fight to Save the Mills	35
Red Cross Responds to Appeals for Help	36
Neighboring Towns Welcome Refugees	37
CHAPTER 4: THE DULUTH FIRES	**43**
Duluth Is Threatened by the Fire	43
Pike Lake	44
Outlying Areas of Duluth	45
Duluth is Saved	46
CHAPTER 5: ISLANDS OF FLAMES	**49**
The Moose Lake/Kettle River Fire Areas	49
Tamarack	50
Lawler	51
Flames in Automba	52
Kettle River Burns	53

Dead Man's Curve	55
Eckman's Corner	56
The Fire in Moose Lake	56

CHAPTER 6: AFTER THE FIRE — **61**

Cloquet Is Destroyed	61
The Minnesota Home Guard, Motor Corps, and National Guard	61
The Duluth Armory and the Red Cross	63
Minnesota Fires Relief Commission	64
Cloquet Jobs Restored	65
Homes Rebuilt	67
Cloquet Schools Reopened	68
Trees Replanted	69
Fond du Lac Ojibwe Receive Relief	69
Rebuilding in the Region	70
Fire Losses Brought to Court	72

GLOSSARY — **77**
NOTES TO THE TEXT — **79**
BIBLIOGRAPHY — **83**
FIRE STORIES — **85**

"One Who Then Was A Wee Girl Recalls Cloquet Fire" by An Anonymous Fire Survivor	85
"Fire Sufferers Remember" by Ada Martin Blinn	89
"Prize Essay Recalls Fire Horrors on Anniversary" by Mrs. Herb (Pearl) Drew	92
"History of Cloquet" by Joseph N. Franklin	97
"Saima's Story" by Saima Lumppio	99
"Memories of the Fire" by Larry Luukkonen	101
"Night of Flame" by Tina Pearson	104
"My Great Aunt" by Katie Casperson	107
"The Wedding" by Beatrice Gellerman	109
Anna Dickie Olesen's Speech Before Congress	112

REMEMBERING THE FIRES — **117**
SUGGESTED READINGS — **121**
NEWSPAPER HEADLINES — **123**
ABOUT THE AUTHORS — **127**

ABOUT THIS BOOK

The publication of this book grew out of a project to design a curriculum that could be used in the Cloquet Public Schools to help in teaching elementary students about the Great Fires of 1918. The curriculum design project was initiated by teachers Kris Sweetnam and Kim Peddle and was partially funded by the Cloquet Educational Foundation. With the 85th anniversary of the fires occurring in 2003, the Carlton County Historical Society Board decided the material should be expanded and published as a book that would be suitable for younger readers, as well as an adult audience wishing an overview of the fire material. Although a number of books have been written about the fire, no previous publication has been done with this audience in mind.

We are indebted to the research and writing of Dr. Francis Carroll and Franklin Raiter who published the book, *The Fires of Autumn: The Cloquet-Moose Lake Disaster of 1918*, for the Minnesota Historical Society Press in 1990. *Fires of Autumn* is still the definitive study of the fires and we have drawn on their material for *Fire Storm*. We are grateful to Francis Carroll for donating the original research material to the Carlton County Historical Society where we have been able to use it in the preparation of this book.

We would like to thank the Moose Lake Area Historical Society and the Minnesota Historical Society for use of photographs from their collections. Many thanks go to Roberta Malwitz for her valuable assistance with the manuscript.

The Cloquet Educational Foundation has generously supported the publication of this book and its distribution in Cloquet schools. We are grateful to Sappi Paper of Cloquet for the donation of paper used in the printing of the book and to those businesses, organizations, and individuals who provided support for the project.

It is our hope that *Fire Storm* will introduce a new generation of readers to the story of these events so crucial to the history of the area. Indeed history here is often spoken of as occurring "before the fire" or "after the fire." As the time of the fires grows more distant and the survivors of the fires fewer, it becomes even more important to tell of the events of the fires and the brave survivors who rebuilt their communities.

Marlene Wisuri, Director
Carlton County Historical Society

ABBREVIATIONS USED:

CCHS ~ Carlton County Historical Society
MLAHS ~ Moose Lake Area Historical Society
MHS ~ Minnesota Historical Society (materials used with permission)

The water pump remains in this scene of destruction.

Telephone poles and fence posts have been burned in the middle.

Photo by Hugh McKenzie from the collection of CCHS

DULUTH HERALD

October 14, 1918.

The so-called Spanish Influenza epidemic was raging around the world at the time of the fires. The flu caused more deaths than the total number of lives lost in World War I.

Schools were closed and articles such as this one from the Duluth Herald gave people information on how to deal with the flu.

Many people in the fire areas, weakened by their ordeals in the fires, died of the Spanish Influenza in the days and weeks following the fires.

SPANISH INFLUENZA--WHAT IT IS AND HOW IT SHOULD BE TREATED

Nothing New—Simply the Old Grip, or La Grippe, That Was Epidemic in 1889-90, Only Then It Came From Russia By Way of France and This Time By Way of Spain.

Go to Bed and Stay Quiet, Take a Laxative—Eat Plenty of Nourishing Food—Keep Up Your Strength—Nature Is the "Cure."

ALWAYS CALL A DOCTOR

NO OCCASION FOR PANIC.

Spanish influenza, which appeared in Spain in May, has all the appearance of grip or la grippe, which has swept over the world in numerous epidemics as far back as history runs. Hippocrates refers to an epidemic in 412 B. C. which is regarded by many to have been influenza. Every century has had its attacks. Beginning with 1831, this country has had five epidemics, the last in 1889-90.

There is no occasion for panic—influenza itself has a very low percentage of fatalities—not over one death out of every four hundred cases, according to the N. C. Board of Health. The chief danger lies in complications arising, attacking principally patients in a run-down condition—those who don't go to bed soon enough, or those who get up too early.

THE SYMPTOMS.

Grippe, or influenza as it is now called, usually begins with a chill, followed by aching, feverishness and sometimes nausea and dizziness, and a general feeling of weakness and depression. The temperature is from 100 to 104, and the fever usually lasts from three to five days. The germs attack the mucous membrane, or lining of the air passages—nose, throat and bronchial tubes—there is usually a hard cough, especially bad at night, often times a sore throat or tonsilitis, and frequently all the appearances of a severe head cold.

THE TREATMENT.

Go to bed at the first symptoms, not only for your own sake but to avoid spreading the disease to others—take a purgative, eat plenty of nourishing food, remain perfectly quiet and don't worry. Quinine, aspirin or Dover's Powder, etc., may be administered by the physician's directions to relieve the aching. But there is no cure or specific for influenzas—the disease must run its course, but nature will throw off the attack if only you keep up your strength. The chief danger lies in the complications which may arise. Influenza so weakens the bodily resistance that there is danger of pneumonia or bronchitis developing, and sometimes inflammation of the middle ear, or heart affections. For these reasons, it is very important that the patient remain in bed until his strength returns—stay in bed at least two days or more after the fever has left you, or if you are over 50 or not strong, stay in bed four days or more, according to the severity of the attack.

EXTERNAL APPLICATIONS.

In order to stimulate the lining of the air passages to throw off the grippe germs, to aid in loosening the phlegm and keeping the air passages open, thus making the breathing easier, Vick VapoRub will be found effective. Hot, wet towels should be applied over the throat, chest and back between the shoulder blades to open the pores. Then VapoRup should be rubbed in over the parts until the skin is red, spread on thickly and covered with two thicknesses of hot flannel cloths. Leave the clothing loose around the neck as the heat of the body liberates the ingredients in the form of vapors. These vapors, inhaled with each breath, carry the medication directly to the parts affected. At the same time, VapoRub is absorbed through and stimulates the skin, attracting the blood to the surface, and thus aids in relieving the congestion within.

HOW TO AVOID THE DISEASE.

Evidence seems to prove that this is a germ disease, spread principally by human contact; chiefly through coughing, sneezing or spitting. So avoid persons having colds—which means avoiding crowds—common drinking cups, roller towels, etc. Keep up your bodily strength by plenty of exercise in the open air, and good food. Above all, keep free from colds, as colds irritate the lining of the air passages and render them much better breeding places for the germs.

Use Vick's VapoRub at the very first sign of a cold. For a head cold, melt a little VapoRub in a spoon and inhale the vapors, or better still, use VapoRub in a benzoin steam kettle. If this is not available, use an ordinary teakettle. Fill half full of boiling water, put in half a teaspoon of VapoRub from time to time—keep the kettle just slowly boiling and inhale the steam arising.

Note. Vick's VapoRub is the discovery of a North Carolina druggist, who found how to combine, in salve form, Menthol and Camphor with such volatile oils as Eucalyptus, Thyme, Cubebs, etc., so that when the salve is applied to the body heat these ingredients are liberated in the form of vapors.

VapoRub is comparatively new in New York state and New England and a few Western states where it is just now being introduced, but in the other sections of the country it is the standard home remedy in over a million homes for all forms of cold troubles. Over six million jars were sold last year. It is particularly recommended for children's croup or colds, since it is externally applied and therefore can be used as freely as desired without the slightest harmful effects. VapoRub can be had in three sizes at all druggists.

INTRODUCTION

October 12, 1918, marked the date of a fiery ordeal for the people of northern Minnesota. A series of great fires swept through towns and rural areas in southern St. Louis, Pine, and Carlton Counties. The fires also burned over areas in Aitkin, Itasca, Cass, Crow Wing, and Wadena counties.

It was the worst disaster to ever happen in Minnesota as far as the total number of lives lost and in property destroyed. The area burned covered 1,500 square miles. The towns of Cloquet, Brookston, Moose Lake, Automba, Kettle River, and at least five others were completely destroyed. In all between 32 to 38 towns or villages were totally or partly burned. Of the 52,371 people that were affected; 11,382 individuals lost their homes, 453 people died, 106 people died from flu and pneumonia immediately after the fire, and 2,100 people were treated for injuries. Property loss was estimated to be about 30 million dollars. It included 4,089 houses, 6,366 barns, 41 school buildings, 54,083 chickens, and 4,295 animals.[1]

In Cloquet, the fire destroyed nearly every building in town; leaving only three sawmills, the Garfield School, a few buildings on Dunlap Island, and several homes standing. Over 8,000 people in Cloquet escaped the flames by taking one of the four trains kept at the city's train depot. The greatest loss of life occured in southern Carlton County where over 200 people lost their lives in the Moose Lake area, between seventy five and one hundred people died at "Dead Man's Curve" near Kettle River, and many were burned or suffocated in wells and root cellars in the rural areas. Several communities north and east of Duluth were burned with the loss of over 100 lives—most in the Pike Lake area.

Since the United States was preoccupied with their men fighting the battles of World War I, most Americans did not even learn of the Cloquet/Moose Lake Fire of 1918. This was also the time of the worldwide epidemic of Spanish Influenza, a life threatening flu that turned into pneumonia. More deaths resulted from this flu than the total number of lives lost in World War I. The crisis was so critical that even schools were closed. As a result, the nation did little or nothing to help the people who survived the fire. What help was given depended upon local people and organizations such as the Red Cross.

The stories of how and where the "The Great Fires of 1918" began, its path throughout northern Minnesota, the escape from the flames, and the help given to the fire survivors is told in this book. Stories by and about fire survivors as well as newspaper articles are included.

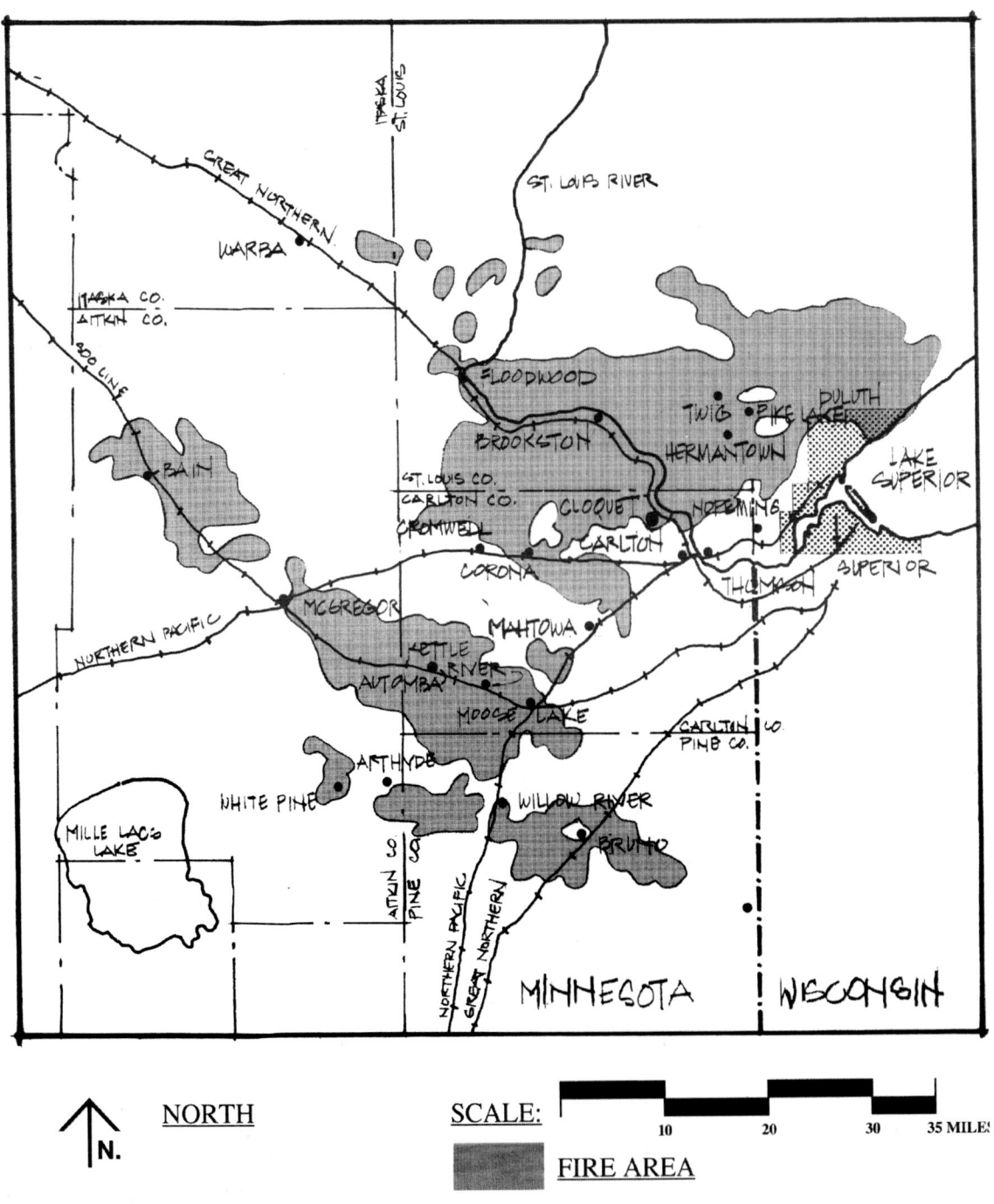

Range of the Fire Areas of the Great Fires of 1918
Map courtesy of Damberg, Scott, Peck & Booker

DATA CONCERNING

the

Minnesota Forest Fires

OCTOBER, 1918.

Irregular spots on map show area burned over, approximately	1,500	sq Miles
Scattered over a territory of	8,400	" "
Families registered	11,382	
Number of people affected	52,371	
Houses destroyed	4,089	
Barns destroyed	6,366	
School buildings	41	
Number of people burned to death	453	
Number of people seriously burned	85	
Number of persons who died from Flu and Pneumonia immediately after the fire	106	
Number of injured who received treatment	2,100	
Number of animals burned	4,295	
Chickens burned	54,083	
Total number of animals requiring feed from Oct. 12 to June 1, 1919, after culling out scrub stock	9,016	
Total loss, over	$30,000,000	

> This information about the fires of 1918 is reproduced from the Final Report of the Minnesota Forest Fires Relief Commission published in 1921. The report was submitted to the Governor of the State of Minnesota.

A railroad track winds through a stand of white pines. Such logging railroads were common in the fire areas.

Photo from the collection of CCHS

CHAPTER ONE
BEFORE THE FIRE

Conditions

The conditions leading to a catastrophic fire were in the making for many months and even years before the Fires of 1918 happened. Nineteen eighteen was a very dry year in northern Minnesota. In fact, it was the driest summer on record in 46 years. Usually this area received a total of 26 inches of rainfall in one year. By October only 6 inches of rain had fallen—a staggering 20 inches less than the normal amount.[2]

The humidity dropped sharply to a low of 21% on October 12th.[3] Even a relative humidity (the amount of moisture or water content in the air) reading at 30% indicates that the air is dry. This meant a drying affect on the forest similar to a dry sponge soaking up water. Studies today have shown that drops in humidity are considered a main factor in large forest fires.[4]

Surrounding the city of Cloquet and throughout Carlton County stood the majestic white pine forests. These trees grew 15-30 inches in diameter (width) and up to 90 feet in height at the turn of the century.[5] The trees and the slashings (branches and other waste) left from the logging of the trees provided a tremendous supply of fuel for a fire.

In addition to the standing timber were the stacks of lumber drying in the yards of the great sawmills in Cloquet and other smaller sawmills such as those in Automba. In Cloquet an estimated 105 million board feet of lumber between the Northern Lumber Company and the Cloquet Lumber Company were drying in their yards at the time of the fire.[6]

Lumberjacks using a two-man saw and an axe to log white pine in Carlton County. The trees could grow up to 90 feet in height.

Photo from the collection of CCHS

15 Fire Storm: The Great Fires of 1918

The conditions which led to the great fires in southern Carlton County were different from the Cloquet Fire in some important ways. A major difference was the presence of numerous peat bogs. Peat, a soil that is in the process of becoming coal, is often used as a fuel. Once it catches on fire it is extremely difficult to put out. It is even known to smolder (to burn with little smoke and no flame) and burn throughout the winter months. Fires as early as the first week in August were spotted in the peat bogs near Moose Lake. These fires smoldered for months until the high winds and low relative humidity on October 12th caused the fire to flair up.

Fires smoldered in peat bogs where they were very difficult to put out.

Photo from the collection of CCHS

A second difference was the presence of virgin pine forests throughout this rural area. At the time of the fire, these forests supplied many small sawmills in the towns of Lawler, Automba, Kettle River, and Moose Lake. The large piles of lumber stored in the yards of the sawmills, along with the piles of sawdust were great sources of fuel for the fire.[7]

Lastly, there were no large lakes or rivers such as the St. Louis River to stop the fires from spreading, although a chain of small lakes in the Moose Lake to Sturgeon Lake area helped to stop the fires from spreading even further.

The stage for a fire was set on the afternoon of October 12th as winds began to pick up. A fall breeze of 20 to 30 miles an hour is enough to fan a small fire. But by 3:00 p.m. that day it had increased to 30 to 40 miles per hour. Such conditions cause a fire to grow and grow and create its own fire weather. The fire begins to suck more fresh air into the base of the large burning area to provide oxygen. As the heat increases, a column of rising flames and smoke rises like a chimney. "The chimney effect" of the column becomes more violent; burning particles, embers, and flaming pine cones or firebrands, are drawn up into the air from the fire itself and blown some distance ahead of the fire. These "firebrands" can create new fires. When several columns of fire join to form flames that reach eight to twelve feet high, a crown fire (fire that explodes into the tops of the trees) can occur. It can also create unusual appearances such as "sheets of flame roiling (violently agitated) overhead, balls of fire descending from the sky, or surges of flames shooting out horizontally from clouds of smoke."[8]

Lack of Safety and Prevention Practices

At the turn of the century there were few fire safety or prevention practices. For example, every fall farmers would clear their fields by burning brush and any leftover garden crops. Although required by law to burn slash, the logging companies often did not burn the slash (branches and other matter left on a forest floor after the cutting of timber) in the cutover lands.

Railroad companies often ignored safety practices, and became key contributors to large forest fires. One of their safety features to prevent fires was to keep a wire-mesh screen or "spark arrestor" over the locomotive's smokestack to stop large pieces of burning coal from getting out. However, this screen was often removed to allow the train to get the power needed to climb a steep hill. This unsafe practice allowed chunks of coal to be thrown out from the smokestack. The hot coals could then easily ignite tall grass alongside the railroad tracks.

Smoke pours from the smoke stack of this Great Northern ore train.

It is thought sparks or burning coals from a train started the fire at Milepost 62 near Brookston.

Photo from the collection of CCHS

Fires caused by the railroads also resulted from their practice of burning grass, garbage, and old railroad ties alongside the railroad tracks (right-of-way). Even though the law in Minnesota at the time of the 1918 fires required the railroad companies to patrol and fight any reported fires along their tracks, they frequently ignored the law.

Lack of Fire Fighting Equipment, Supplies, & Trained Firefighters

There was little in the way of fire fighting equipment, supplies, and trained firefighters in 1918. For the most part fires were fought with simple hand tools—a shovel, an axe, a hoe, and back pumps. There were no hi-tech airplanes capable of scooping large amounts of water from lakes; nor were there airtankers to drop flame-retardant (resistant to catching fire) chemicals to put out forest fires. They did not have the helicopters we have today that can fly at rates of 100 miles per hour and that are on standby (immediate readiness) in five locations throughout the state. Nor did they have fire trucks with tall ladders which could reach tall multi-storied buildings such as mills, hospitals, and apartments. They did not have the fire trucks used today that have the capability of pumping 1,250 gallons of water per minute. There were no bulldozers to build firebreaks. Natural obstacles such as roads, rivers, and lakes were used to contain the fire.[9]

Unlike the paid firefighters we see today, fire fighting in 1918 depended largely upon volunteers. Added to this problem was a lack of available men to fight the fire as many of them were overseas fighting in World War I.

Lack of an Effective Communication System

In 1918 area fire departments lacked the Central Dispatch system—the 911 number—which provides immediate response to emergencies. This means of communication used today allows the fire department to work as a team with police and hospitals so that together they can react with speed, efficiency, and services in an emergency.

Fire Storm: The Great Fires of 1918 18

These four pictures are details from a panoramic photograph taken of Cloquet before the fire by Olaf Olson. It shows the many stacks of drying lumber stockpiled in the city.

Photos from the collection of CCHS

Cloquet was a thriving city of almost 8,000 people before the fire. Lumber mills, the Northwest Paper Company, the match mill, and the box factory provided jobs for a largely immigrant work force.

CHAPTER TWO

THE CLOQUET FIRE BEGINS

Milepost 62

The great fire that destroyed Cloquet started as a railroad fire along the Great Northern Railway tracks at Milepost 62. This was four miles northwest of Brookston on the banks of the St. Louis River and fifteen miles northwest of Cloquet.

At about 4:30 in the afternoon on October 10, 1918, a passenger train on its way from Duluth to Hibbing stopped at a siding called "O'Brien's Spur" at Milepost 62. A siding is a loading station where large amounts of wood products are piled on a large platform until they are moved to another place to be sold. O'Brien's Spur siding was about 2,000 feet long and held as much as 10,000 cords (one cord equals a stack of wood measuring 4 by 4 by 8 feet) of pulpwood, cordwood, railroad ties, fence posts, and telephone poles.[10]

A railroad siding on a logging railroad. A steam driven log loader is loading cut logs onto a railroad car.

Photo from the collection of CCHS

A farmer by the name of Steve Koskela and his neighbor, John Sundstrom, were collecting ties at the siding for Koskela's barn. They spotted smoke rising from the western end of the siding just as the train left. When they approached the smoke they found a fire about twenty feet across burning through the tall, dry, grass near the piles of wood. Having no tools to stop the fire, they watched as it spread under a pile of cordwood at the siding. Koskela went home to get pails and shovels and also recruit his neighbors to help fight the fire. With the help of his neighbors they worked late into the night trying to stop the fire but couldn't put it out.[11]

On the following day, Friday, October 11th, Koskela and several crews continued to fight the fire. Later that day the crewmen left to work in Brookston leaving Koskela alone to battle the fire. The weather conditions got worse as a large body of cold air moved into the area bringing with it a dry northwest wind and a record-breaking fall in

21   Fire Storm: The Great Fires of 1918

humidity. All of these weather conditions added to the fast rate at which the fire was able to spread.

About 11:30 on Saturday morning Koskela was returning from a shopping errand in Brookston when he saw the siding at O'Brien's Spur completely surrounded with flames. It was apparent that the dried wood on the siding provided a large amount of fuel for the fire to get out of control.[12]

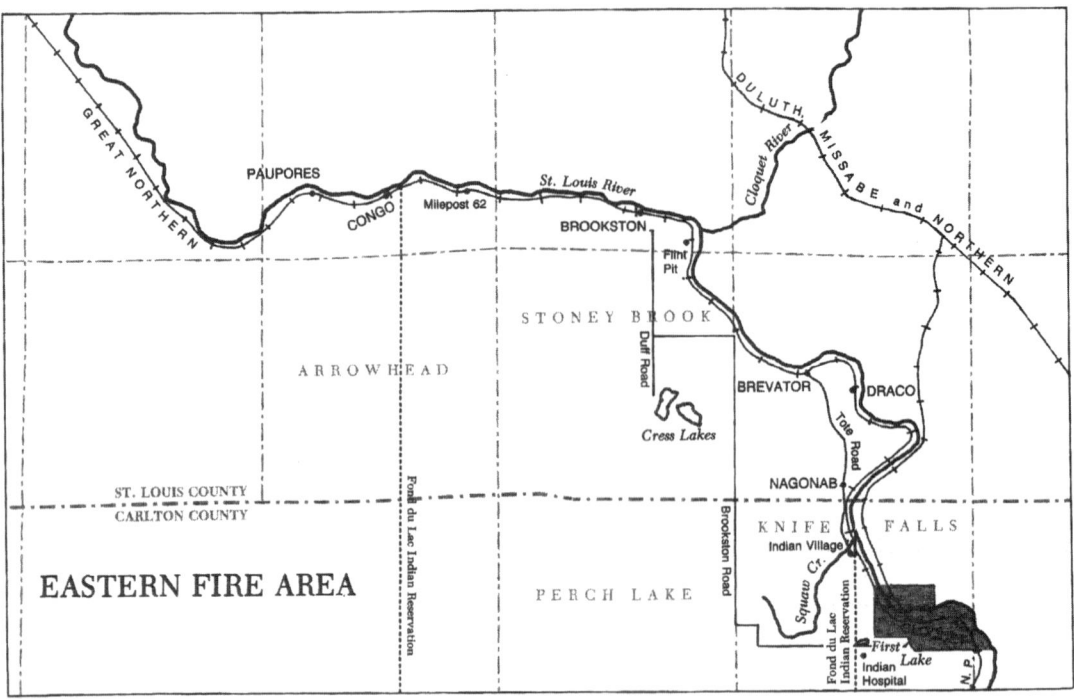

This map of the Eastern Fire Area shows milepost 62 on the Great Northern railroad tracks west of Brookston. It was from this location that the Cloquet Fire spread to Cloquet, Hermantown, and the areas surrounding the city of Duluth.

Map reproduced from Fires of Autumn, Minnesota Historical Society Press.

Koskela rushed home as he knew his farm was in danger of being destroyed by the fire. He quickly gathered whatever cash he had at home (needed to buy food and other supplies if his home burned). With the help of his family they took pails of water to wet down their buildings and opened the doors of the barns so the animals were free to escape from the fire. The fire reached his home by 1:40 p.m. Within the next hour Koskela was able to save his home and family but lost many of his other buildings and supplies.[13]

Koskela's neighbors were not as fortunate. The Knuttis, who lived about a half mile east of Koskela, lost their home to the fire. They became the first refugees (people who are fleeing from danger and seeking a place that provides protection or shelter) of the fire and were able to find help at the Koskela home.[14]

The full force of the fire reached Brookston, a town of about 500 people, around 2:00 in the afternoon. During the next two hours the wind increased in strength to about ten miles an hour as it traveled from a northwest to southeast direction. The sun appeared red in the sky, the air was thick with smoke, and the heat from the fire was so great that it caused homes to burst into flames even before the fire reached the town from the west.[15]

By 4:10 in the afternoon the Brookston village president, Charles DeWitt, and over 200 of his townspeople boarded the Great Northern freight train. In order to flee the fire which was traveling from the northwest, the train headed seventeen miles southeast to the city of Cloquet.[16]

The small town of Brookston is pictured before the fire and after it was destroyed by the flames.

Photos from the collection of CCHS

The freight trains, which typically carried cargo such as lumber and farming goods, were now called "relief trains." The reason for this was that the trains would provide help (relief) by carrying the people out of the fire danger to a place of shelter and safety.

About a mile south of Brookston at "Flint Pit," the relief train was surrounded by flames and the refugees were scorched. Elizabeth McCamus Johnson recalls, "The flames were leaping over the tops of our cars. The train was going through walls of fire."[17]

By 5:00 p.m. the scorched Great Northern train arrived in Cloquet with over 200 blackened and distressed refugees. They were the first sign to the people of Cloquet of the great danger and possible need to evacuate.

Fond du Lac Indian Reservation

The fire swept in a southeast direction from Milepost 62 to the Fond du Lac Indian Reservation. Between 7:00 to 7:30 p.m. it reached the Indian village overlooking the St. Louis River where it destroyed everything in its path. While many of the Brookston people were able to board the relief train to Cloquet, the Ojibwe Indians in the northern area of the Fond du Lac Reservation lived further inland and did not have access to the railroads. They had to find another means of escape. Many took refuge in the rivers. This is what one woman had to say: "[We] had the common sense that God gave [us] to go to the river like an animal. All the animals were there. There were bears swimming out there."[18]

Fire refugees from the Fond du Lac Reservation pictured beside one of the tents that were distributed to shelter fire survivors.

Photo from the collection of CCHS

Still others sought refuge in the lakes. Mrs. Grace Sheehy who lived on a farm on the Duff Road recalls her experience:

> The flames had crossed the road, so they turned around, walked a mile south toward Cress Lakes (also called Twin Lakes). At about 5:00 p.m. they could see fire burning heavily to the north and west of them. They found a boat on the edge of the western lake, and Beargrease paddled them out onto the water. From the boat they could see fire all around them . . . but the fire at the lake did not burn all the shoreline . . . About 8:00 p.m. Beargrease brought the boat in to shore.[19]

Fire Storm: The Great Fires of 1918 24

However, the lakes were not always a place of safety. Eva Alberg who lived in western Carlton County had this to say:

> The heat was so intense that while the fire itself was still about a mile away, our home which was covered with tar paper exploded into flames! All the fish in Dutch and Sandabacka Lakes west of us cooked and those who took refuge in their boats—the children and those barefooted—got blisters on the bottom of their feet because the water got so hot as the fire rolled into the lakes.[20]

Then there were those like the Petite family who chose to take the road into Cloquet. About 4:00 p.m. Joseph Petite recalled seeing heavy smoke in the northwest as he was picking the vegetables out of his garden. By 7:00 p.m. the smoke was so close that he and his wife decided to leave their farm and walk the old road to the Indian Village (the largest of the Ojibwe settlements on the Indian reservation). By the time they reached the village there was no one there. Sparks were raining down on them. They now knew that they could not stay there overnight and must continue their way south to Cloquet. As they reached the riverbank where the Northern Lumber Company stood on the west side of Cloquet, flaming pinecones called firebrands were flying all over them. Petite remembers them being as big as balls.[21]

Father Simon walks among the ruins of the Catholic Mission on the Fond du Lac Reservation on October, 15, 1918.

Photo from St. John's Abbey Archive

Despite the fact that the entire Indian village was destroyed, the Indians fared the best when it came to survival. Reports indicate that at most, only one life was lost.

25 Fire Storm: The Great Fires of 1918

Rural Areas Are Ablaze

The fire rushed onward into rural areas surrounding Cloquet and Duluth. At the Luomala farm in Saginaw, the family frantically hitched their horses to a long, heavy potato wagon. This is what Katharine Luomala had to say:

> Even when we had left the yard, there had not been much fire about us, but now it suddenly swept about us until the whole world was on fire. Every tree on both sides of the road, every fence post, every stump, and every blade of grass was ablaze. Red flashes of flame skimmed up the trees and jumped across the branches which fell crashing to earth. The fence posts were rows of burning torches. The thick underbrush of the roadside was burning fiercely, and brands of fire fell into the road. The terrified horses dodged around them and galloped on. I expected any minute to be swept heavenward in a blazing wagon drawn by two snorting horses.[22]

Numerous farms were burned in all of the fire areas. Barns, farm machinery, crops, and cattle were lost. Members of many farm families also perished in the rural areas.

Photo by St. Paul Dispatch from the collection of MHS

The fire which started at Milepost 62 spread to the areas surrounding the city of Duluth. The fire jumped to the east bank of the St. Louis River south of Brookston shortly after 4:00 p.m. and burst into flames traveling both north and south along the river. Meanwhile to the north, a gravel train on the Duluth, Missabe and Northern line started fires along the railroad tracks between Culver and Alborn. Railroad workers and local people attempted to put out the fires there and an effort was made again to stop the fire at the Stony Brook road, but the fires quickly got out of control all along the tracks and began burning farms in the area.[23]

This well known photograph of the ruins of Cloquet soon after the fire was taken by Cloquet photographer, Olaf Olson. The old water tower provides a landmark in the devastated city. The ruins of the Weyerhaeuser home is in the lower left corner of the photo with only the chimney left standing.

Photo from the collection of CCHS

A new public high school had been built in Cloquet and was less than one year old at the time of the fire. This photograph shows all that was left of the school after the fire. A new school was built in the same location at the corner of Fifth Street and Carlton Avenue. It is now Cloquet's Middle School. Of all of the schools in Cloquet, only Garfield School survived the fire.

Photo by Olaf Olson from the collection of CCHS

Cloquet's Public Library was destroyed by the flames. It was rebuilt in the same place and dedicated on the anniversary of the fire in 1920. It now serves as the home of the Carlton County Historical Society.

Photo by Hugh McKenzie from the collection of CCHS

CHAPTER THREE

THE FIRE ENTERS CLOQUET

The City Is Alerted to the Approaching Fire

In the middle of the afternoon smoke could be seen and smelled in the city of Cloquet. At first, the townspeople were not alarmed as small fires were a common occurrence. Slash left in the cutover lands, the garden remains from the harvest, and old railroad ties were typically set on fire at this time of year. Besides, they were busy with harvesting and canning the vegetables from their gardens as well as laying in a supply of firewood and coal to heat their homes in winter. Even when the distressed refugees from Brookston arrived in Cloquet to inform them that Cloquet would soon be doomed, few believed it possible.

Around 7:00 p.m. Rudolph Weyerhaeuser, manager of the Northern Lumber Company, and Northern Lumber Company secretary, Sherman Coy, arrived in Cloquet after spending a business day in the Twin Cities. Coy, who had just finished having supper with the Weyerhaeuser's in Cloquet, decided to head for town to learn of the latest news of the fire. After walking a block he turned around. This is what he saw:

> I saw a huge sheet of flame over the hill back of his [Weyerhaeuser's] house a short distance away. I turned to go back immediately and he followed. We went over the hill by our garden and into the ravine yard. The fire was then only a few feet from the lumber piles. I turned in the alarm from the box right there and then ran to the pump house for full pressure, and had the engineer blow the siren, and keep it up.[24]

The heightened alert could now be felt throughout the city as mill sirens rang and steam whistles blew continuously. This signaled the shutting down of the mills and the entry of the fire into the city.

Rudolph Weyerhaeuser watched as the flames ignited the piles of lumber drying in the yards of the Northern Lumber Company. Quickly he gathered four other men to help him stop the fire. Watering the fire with their two hoses soon became hopeless as the fire hastened through the mill, the planer, and over 65 million board feet of dry lumber in the yards. Within minutes the fire raced out of control as the 65 to 85 miles per hour wind hurled the boards like flaming torches across the city. The fate of the city was clear. The mass exodus would soon begin.[25]

The Townspeople Prepare to Leave

News to evacuate the city reached the townspeople in many ways. For some it was a phone call from a loved one. Ada Martin Blinn recalls the phone call from her son Ned, "Pack a few things and prepare to leave at once. The fire is very near. Pack a grip (suitcase) with things that [you] would need most for a few days—a bundle of bedding, a warm quilt and your winter coat."[26]

Others received phone calls from one of the two switchboard operators. Acting on the orders given by Mayor John Long to call every phone number in the city, they worked tirelessly throughout the evening until the last relief train left the station.[27]

Many received the news to prepare to leave when their father was sent home from the sawmills. Rosella Harney recalls that moment when her father, Conrad Singpiel, Sr., ran home from the mills:

> Yelling and screaming as loudly as he could. He told my mother to grab us kids and get down to the railroad depot as fast as we could as the whole town was on fire. Mother was very upset because we couldn't find Dutch. Father told her there was no time to look for him. [28]

For some it was a "Paul Revere town crier" racing up and down the streets on horseback shouting and urging people to "HURRY TO THE DEPOT, CLOQUET IS ON FIRE."[29] Likewise Mayor John Long sent runners and the four man police force throughout the city with the same message.[30]

The questions now on everyone's mind were, "What should I pack and how should I escape? Should I go by foot, by train, or by car?"

Escape by Train

The railroads became the means by which most of the population found safety. If it had not been for their timely assistance, there is little question that the loss of life would have been greater. The success of the trains moving nearly 8,000 refugees out of town is largely due to the foresight and heroic efforts of a man by the name of Lawrence

Fauley. He was the Cloquet depot agent at the time of the fire. As soon as he heard of the flight of the Brookston refugees he made plans to get as many empty railroad cars as possible to Cloquet. He was unable to get approval from his bosses to carry out this order as it was Saturday and the offices were closed. Nevertheless, Fauley took it upon himself to line up as many empty cars as he could get. With incredible foresight he diverted all trains that might have blocked the refugee trains from getting out.[31]

As hundreds of townspeople hurriedly walked from their homes toward the depot it was not surprising to see them carrying something in their arms—perhaps a quilt, a coat, a favorite doll, or grandma's treasured heirloom. Once they arrived at the depot platform they were ushered to railroad freight cars.

There was no talking. Only the voices of the men who were doing the loading could be heard. "This way"—"Give me your hand"—"How many?"—"No room for baby buggies"—"I will help you." Many of the small children were tied chainwise to each other at the wrist so they would not stray and be lost amidst the heavy smoke and crowds.[32]

Depot agent, Lawrence Fauley, is credited for lining up trains and railroad cars to evacuate the city of Cloquet. Many lives were saved because of his quick thinking.

This is the depot in Cloquet where men, women, and children were loaded into railroad cars and taken from the city the night of October 12th.

Photos from the collection of CCHS

31 Fire Storm: The Great Fires of 1918

Men, women, and children could be seen climbing up the little steps into the railroad freight cars. Many of these cars were very dirty because they had been used to transport iron ore or coal. Yells could be heard "all men and boys over sixteen stay back and fight the fire."[33] For the refugees it seemed like an endless wait for the trains to move.

As each person came aboard the refugees would hear of how much closer the fire was. Thoughts of "Why can't we go?" or "How many more people do they think they can pack into our coach?" was on everyone's mind. And once the train did leave, it moved at such a slow pace. Every few blocks it stopped to pick up more refugees.

The refugees were taken to various cities depending on which of the four trains they boarded. If they were aboard the first train, a three-coach passenger Great Northern train carrying over 1,000 people, they would arrive in Carlton and then in Superior. If they were aboard the two Great Northern ore trains, made up of 4,700 people, they would arrive in Superior. And if they boarded the mixed freight and ore cars of the Northern Pacific train, made up of 2,000 passengers, they would arrive in Duluth.[34]

The people who boarded the first train (often called Gilbert's train for it was named after the conductor) faced much difficulty that evening and in the days to follow. Being that only women and children were allowed on this train many families became separated. This was a problem for many as the trains were destined to arrive in different towns.[35]

The trains offered little comfort. There were no seats, blankets, or pillows. Those fleeing did not "dare stick their noses out, as the atmosphere was dense with smoke and unbelievably hot."[36] If you were one of the lucky ones you sat on a bundle of whatever you brought instead of the bottom of the car. Evelyn Elshoss recalls the discomfort of her ride:

> I can see myself sitting in a corner of the boxcar. Bodies are packed together all about me. My nostrils are filled with the stench of the barnyard, of too permeating perfumes, of unbathed bodies, of garlic, and of tobacco.. [I could hear] murmured prayers and childish whimperings.[37]

The difficulties brought on by the cold of the night in the middle of October were felt by many. Comments such as "I wish I had taken my overcoat." or "My head is so cold." could be heard.[38] However, with the difficulties, also came acts of kindness. Offers of a small towel and a safety pin improvised for a scarf, a blanket for a coat.

Escape by Foot

While many of the Cloquet residents escaped the fire by train there were some who chose or had no other means to escape except by walking. Many who lived on the east end of the city walked to Carlton by way of 14th Street. This road became so crowded that it took about two hours to get to Carlton.[39] Others simply huddled in fields on the outskirts of town. Evelyn Elizabeth Erickson had this to say about her family's climb up the hill back of Dunlap Island:

> From there they saw the town go up in flames, saw the gasoline storage tanks burn, and watched the progress of the fire as it leaped from section to section of the town. Exclamations could be heard such as: "There goes the library." "That's the high school going up in smoke." Or "The City Hall has caught now." Until way past midnight, they sat watching the smoldering ruins. Later they sought shelter in a house on the island.[40]

Escape by Automobile

Although the vast majority of people did not own automobiles, a handful of car owners in town used this means to escape. Often times the car owners provided help for the elderly, the sick, and the handicapped by giving them rides to the trains before they fled for safety. Many took 14th Street which was a main road from Cloquet to Carlton. Others drove to Scanlon, a town about three miles from Cloquet as "it was not in the path of the fire and did not burn."[41]

Mr. and Mrs. Sherman Coy were among those who fled Cloquet by automobile. A newspaper account tells of their escape:

Automobiles such as the one pictured below were becoming somewhat more common by the time of the fire. They proved to be a valuable means of escape from the fire for many people of Cloquet. However many people in other areas died in wrecked and burned automobiles while fleeing the fires.

Photo from the collection of CCHS

33 Fire Storm: The Great Fires of 1918

In an automobile they drove to Carlton, out of the danger zone. Their path led along a road crowded with refugees, some carrying bundles, others with wheelbarrows and some pushing baby carriages...The air was dense with smoke.[42]

Fury of the Flames Sweeps City

With winds gusting from 65 to 85 miles per hour the fire raged into the city about 8:00 p.m. It entered the upper yards of the Northern Lumber Company known as "Bottle Alley." Once this ravine, filled with 65 million board feet of dry lumber ignited, the fire quickly spread beyond control. From the yards of the Northern Lumber Company the fire swept through the West End of the city. Around 9:00 p.m. homes on the hills of Ave. D and Arch Street were among the first to catch on fire. From there it continued its path on the high ridges between Avenue F and Carlton Avenue from 3rd Street down to about 13th Street.[43]

Meanwhile the fire raced onward to Dunlap Island. Here as in other parts of the city the fire's destruction was erratic. How the fury of the flames would destroy one building while another building right

In the aftermath of the fire, Cloquet lay in ruins. A few buildings on Dunlap Island did not burn and can be seen in this photo taken looking north over the west end of Cloquet.

Photo from the collection of CCHS

next to it would be saved is a mystery. While the Duluth and Northeastern Railroad Depot and the St. Louis Mercantile Company on the west side of the island were destroyed; the Northeastern Hotel and several other buildings on the east side were spared. The St. Louis River bridge, next to the island, was also left unharmed.[44]

Across from Dunlap Island the fire entered the yards of the Cloquet Lumber Company. By 10:00 p.m. the flames continued its warlike destruction of the businesses along Cloquet Avenue. Without care or concern it marched onward, devouring the train depot and two of the boxcars of the last train. Quickly the burning cars were pulled away from the rest of the train which was loaded with passengers. Sparks from the burning buildings rained down on the train as it moved further up the tracks. By 10:30 p.m. the train left the yards with Mayor Long aboard.[45]

The Harrowing Train Ride

The ride out of the city was not without danger. Pearl Drew who was aboard the first train that left Cloquet for Carlton had this to say of the stressful ride:

> We passed through Carlton, came to the high trestle in Jay Cooke [State] Park, and stopped right in the middle of it. Of all places we had stopped, this seemed the worst. Fire was everywhere—flames licking from the deep gullies to the very tracks we were on. This was the end—we were sure of it. The rails were so hot, they dared not attempt to put the weight of the engine on them, until they were cooled.[46]

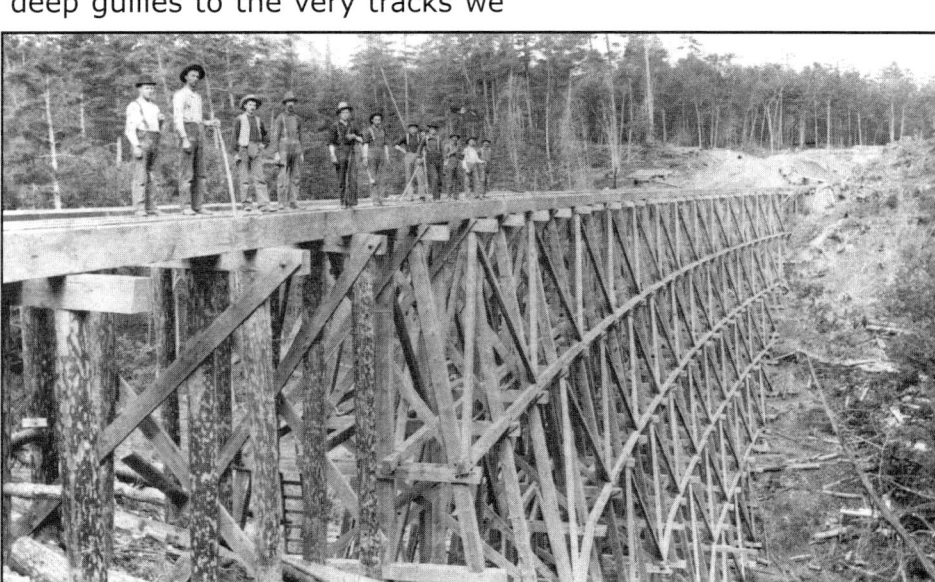

This train trestle is typical of a type that trains crossed escaping the fires. These trestles could be found in several places in Carlton County where the railroads criss-crossed the county.

Photo from the collection of CCHS

Ada Martin Blinn says about her train ride, "We were moving about as fast as a man could walk, every culvert and bridge we passed over was either on fire or had been. . . we were in great danger of a wreck."[47]

The Fight to Save the Mills

Meanwhile about 17 to 50 men stayed back to fight the fire and save the mills. Among them were Rudolph Weyerhaeuser, Henry Hornby, and Joseph Wilson, managers of the three lumber companies.

Manager Weyerhauser and his crew of four men worked tirelessly to save the Northern Lumber Company.[48]

The big sawmill of the Cloquet Lumber Company was saved, although the planing mill and countless board feet of lumber in the storage yard burned.

Photo by Olaf Olson from the collection of CCHS

Although their attempts failed, others had better success. Among them was Manager Hornby of the Cloquet Lumber Company. He along with a crew of men worked throughout the night. Using pumps to draw water from the river, they continuously wet down their plant. Although the planing mill and much of the cut lumber in the storage yards burned, they were successful in saving their big sawmill.[49]

Further down the river at the Johnson-Wentworth Lumber Company, Manager Wilson and his crew of men were able to save most of their plant including the only planing mill that was to survive the fire. The planing mill (a machine that smooths the rough lumber into a smooth surface) would later play an important factor in the rebuilding of the town. Because it was spared, the Johnson-Wentworth Company would become the only source of lumber supply in the city during the rebuilding of the temporary homes.[50]

Red Cross Responds to Appeals for Help

By late afternoon news of the plight of the Brookston refugees and the growing fire crisis had reached the Duluth and Superior Red Cross. The alert heightened as reports came in from the National Guard who had been sent out to fight the fires throughout the day. As soon as Major Weaver of the National Guard returned to Duluth after seeing the town of Cloquet leveled and deserted, he directed Kathleen Covy to set up an emergency hospital in the National Guard dormitory of the Duluth Armory. Without delay she obtained help from the medical corps of the Home Guard to set up cots in long rows. As the evening wore on more medical supplies, bedding, and cots were needed. The Red Cross was able to obtain these needed supplies from local hospitals, hotels, and stores. In addition the Red Cross appealed for trained medical staff to help. Doctors and nurses throughout the city promptly responded. All night and into the next morning refugees streamed into the Duluth Armory.[51] Mrs. W. H. Flavel had this to say:

> We were taken to the Duluth Armory where we were met by nurses who tied masks over our faces [to prevent the Spanish Influenza from spreading]. A hot lunch was served to us in the dining hall, then we were taken to the main floor where cots and blankets were provided for those who cared to use them.[52]

In Duluth and Superior the Red Cross made arrangements to place the overflow of refugees at the courthouse, the YMCA, churches, hotels, and club buildings such as the Masonic temple. At least one doctor and several nurses were assigned to each building.[53]

Neighboring Towns Welcome Refugees

The people in the neighboring towns of Carlton, Superior, and Duluth welcomed the refugees with open arms. They generously provided services and supplies to the fire victims. This could be anything from serving hot meals to providing carloads of clothing, to providing medical assistance for the injured, and to opening their homes, churches, schools, and halls for shelter.

Once the trains arrived at the depot, the refugees could be seen climbing out of the cars as fast as they

Red Cross kitchen workers serve a hot meal to National Guardsmen and fire survivors at Carlton after the fire.

Photo from the collection of MHS

could. However, those who were among the last to get out of the railroad car had the problem of not having a step or person to help them get out. Ada Blinn, a fire survivor, had this to say, "The cars were like being inside of an iron box with sides about six feet high and no doors."[54] Someone already outside of the railroad car would have to find a box or something that could be used as a step.

As the refugees set foot on the depot platform welcoming calls could be heard. "Room for two"—"Room for three."[55] Many of the refugees responded to these invitations and took shelter in those homes that night and in the following days:

> A man said, "Here is a family with a baby—you take them." A deep kindly voice said, "Let me carry the little girl and you people come with me." I remember being carried blocks then into a strange house, and laid on a bed. Then morning—to find grandma in bed with me in this unfamiliar room. I stepped out of the bed only to trip on the adult-size nightgown. Mother came in. "Mama, I want to go home to our house and I want Sally-dolly." "Oh, my darling," sobbed mother, "we have no house, your daddy has no job in the mill. We are homeless."[56]

One of the first things that was done as the refugees unboarded the trains was to have the severely burned and injured taken to the hospitals while the rest were brought to a big hall for lunch. In Carlton more than 800 refugees were cared for at the Odd Fellows Hall and in other buildings under the direction of Rev. Father Kiley, R. Barstow, and the women of the town.[57]

Meanwhile in Duluth most of the refugees were taken to the Duluth National Guard Armory where they were served hot meals prepared by the Home and National Guard. By Sunday they had fed nearly 3,000 fire survivors.[58]

Since the Great Northern and Soo Railroad lines ran from the fire stricken areas into Superior, it became a major site for relief operations. One of the first persons to act on the likelihood of refugees descending on the city was Major George B. Stewart, superintendent of the Great Northern Railroad in Superior. He received reports from his station agents throughout the evening from the fire stricken areas. Knowing that Cloquet was in the path of the fire, he organized relief operations with twenty-four businessmen. By the time the first train of refugees arrived at 11:30 p.m., they were ready with food, medical assistance, and shelter. Among the 18 different buildings used to house the refugees were churches, schools, the YMCA, stores, club buildings, and private homes.[59]

Pearl Drew had this to say of her night spent at the YMCA in Superior:

> I went to the "Y," where volunteers were making thousands of sandwiches and gallons of coffee. Mattresses were spread over the large "gym" floor, each one haven of a foreign family. They would not be separated for a minute. With their few belongings in a sack, the mother clutched it firmly and would not budge. The family moved as a whole, or not at all.[60]

For many of the refugees they had only one thing on their mind—they wanted to find their families or at least to know that they were safe. "Have you seen any of my family?" was the question asked over and over again.[61] How did they find missing family members or loved ones? Many of the telephone and telegraph lines were down and the only way to get news was to go and check the lists of registered refugees posted at businesses, train stations, the Duluth Armory, and other refugee sites. These lists were primarily recorded by over fifty-one American Red Cross social workers sent to the area.[62] The Red Cross took the names and temporary addresses from these lists and had them published in the newspapers so refugees could locate family members.

Marie Lavasseur had this to say of her search:

> There were several business places where people registered. I stopped in so many places with no success that finally I went back to our rooms and found Mother watching, hoping, and praying. So I set out again and late that afternoon I found my brother's signature. It was like finding a gold mine. I located him by telephone. It did not take long for him to find me.[63]

On the evening of Monday, October 13, 1918, the *Duluth Herald* newspaper reported:

> Blasted out and dead is the once thriving city of Cloquet. Swept by a devastating wall of flame which fairly shriveled all in its path within two hours, the residence and business districts of the once thriving City of Pines of 8,000 population were swept clean as a sandy beach. Only a few heaps of crumbled brick mark the spot where but a few hours before a hotel or a store was handling its business, or a residence where everyone was happy and carefree.
>
> Where the enormous lumber yards and residences were there is now but a smooth, barren stretch of gray ashes. Two companies of the Fourth regiment are on guard.
>
> Yet, withall, Cloquet is fortunate. Two-thirds of the industries still remain and are ready to resume work and give employment to hundreds as soon as they return.

The number of refugees that had registered in Superior was 9,039. By the end of October, 3,685 of the 8,375 refugees that had been helped in Superior had left. Among those who stayed behind were 110 burned or injured refugees who remained hospitalized. The number of cases of influenza was 295 with two deaths.[64]

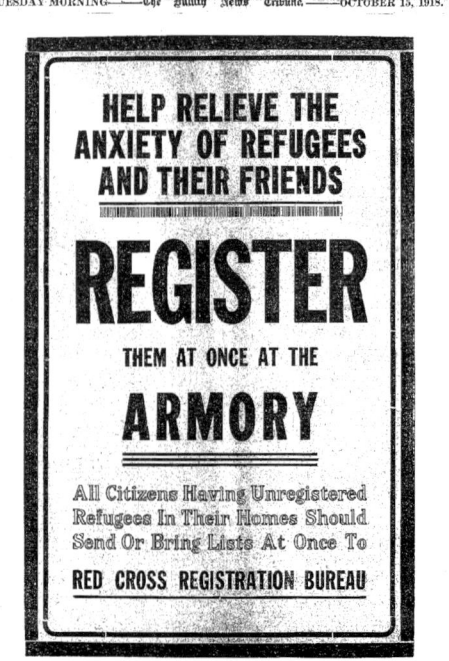

This notice appeared in the Duluth News Tribune *on October 15, 1918. Many fire refugees had become separated from their families during the fire and were very anxious to find their loved ones.*

The Red Cross had a Registration Bureau and kept lists of the survivors.

12 Monday, THE DULUTH HERALD October 14, 1918.

REFUGEES REGISTERED AT RED CROSS HEADQUARTERS AT NEW ARMORY

Virtually all refugees from the holocaust which swept the country north and west of Duluth on Saturday night and Sunday morning, and who have arrived in Duluth, have been registered at Red Cross emergency headquarters at the New Armory. This list is published in the hope that it will prove a guide to those who are seeking lost relatives, and is given herewith:

Ahier, Robert, wife and two children, Cloquet, Minn.
Anderson, Annie, Cloquet, Minn.
Anderson, Mrs. Charles and seven children, Cloquet, Minn.
Anderson, Ener, wife and one child, Cloquet, Minn.
Anderson, Therea, Cloquet, Minn.
Armstrong, A. R., Cloquet, Minn.
Anderson, Mrs. L. Leif, and Roy, 1109 Fifty-first avenue east.
Anderson, Peter, and wife and one daughter, Cloquet, Minn.
Amotozio, Frank, wife and six children.
Anne, E., Forty-seventh avenue east.
Allstad, W., 4505 Cooke street.
Archer, Mrs. Joe, Hoeligen, Lakeside.
Anderson, Peter, and wife, Cloquet, Minn.
Anerson, Andrew, Hutchinson road.
Almen, Peter, and wife, Arnold road.
Addison, Mrs. Winsham.
Anderson, Mrs. Cloquet, Minn.
Abramhamson, Mrs. Charles, Moose Lake (badly burned).
Abramhamson, Ed, Moose Lake (badly burned).
Aattanen, William, Cloquet.
Arthur, Fred, wife and two children, Cloquet.
Aaltonen, William, Cloquet.
Ameli, John, Mrs. and son, Cloquet.
Andersen, Jenny and Roy, 1105 Fifty-first avenue east.
Anderson, John, Agnes and Ernest, 1109 Fifty-first avenue east.
Anderson, N. T., 5125 Tioga street.
Anderson, Mr. and Mrs. Gustave, Lakeside.
Anderson, Eric, wife and two children.
Anderson, Gustave, and wife.
Anderson, Carl, wife and daughter, Homecroft park.
Anderson, Mrs. B. C., Lakeside.
Anderson, Mrs. Andrew, and two children, 5123 Tioga street.
Anderson, Andrew, wife and four children, Brookston.
Archer, Mrs. Joseph, and four children, Colbyville.
Asplund, Erick, wife and four children, Cloquet, Minn.
Asplund, John, wife and three children, Cloquet, Minn.
Arsenau, Alex, 218 East Second street.

Butkiewiecz, Sophia, Cloquet.
Brunneau, Mrs., Duluth Heights.
Burman, Mrs., 48 Sixteenth avenue east.
Bush, Mrs. M. R. and 2 daughters, 5803 East Superior street.
Burke, Thomas and wife, Rice Lake road.
Burke, Tim, wife and daughter, Cloquet.
Burke, John and wife, Cloquet.
Bye, Mrs. Julia, Poor farm.
Buck, Mrs. E. L., 2 boys, Exeter Farms.
Berutsen, Tom, Nora farm.
Browning, Ethel, Homecroft Park.
Broch, Mr. and Mrs. Joseph, and 6 children, Oneida street, Lakeside.
Brown, Harold.
Brawley and wife, R. F. D.
Brayden, Harry, Proctor, Minn.
Boland, Mr. and Mrs. Matt, Brookston.
Bollins, W. L., 112 West Palmetto street.
Boland, Matt and wife, Brookston.
Borgman, Mrs. John and child, 5201 Dodge street.
Bergerin, Ernest, wife and children, Cloquet.
Blikt, John, Cloquet.
Blain, Mrs. John and 2 children, Cloquet.
Berthuime, Frank, wife and 3 children, Cloquet.
Bernier, M. Cloquet.
Bereran, Frank, Cloquet.
Benson, Walter, Cora and Alfred, 3 miles this side of Pike Lake.
Barton, Mrs., Moose Lake.
Bendla, William, Cloquet.
Barrett, wife and 2 children, Cloquet.
Barker, Carl, Cloquet.
Barby, Christ, wife and 2 children, Adolph, Minn.

son, Brookston.
Connors, Mrs. Levi, Cloquet.
Coon, Mrs. M.
Copprud, Christ, Woodland.
Coughlin, Christ, and wife, 4009 West First street.
Corbin, Mrs. Mike, Cloquet.
Cowgan, Mrs., Cloquet.
Crook, A., Cloquet.
Cross, Mrs. Frank, Cloquet.
Cummings, Mrs. J. A., 1522 Jefferson street.
Curry, Dave, Cloquet.
Curry, J. H.
Culford, Stephen, wife and 2 children, 29 Minneapolis avenue.
Czakie, Mrs. George, Cloquet.

Dahl, Edw., wife and 2 children, Cloquet.
Danielson, H. A., 4 children, Cloquet.
Darby, Thos., wife and 4 children, Cloquet.
Delyea, Mrs. Victor T., Cloquet.
Doge, Charles, Cloquet.
Doge, Frank, wife and 2 children, Scanlon.
Dachan, O., and 3 children.
Dahl, Ed., Cloquet.
Dahl, Mrs. and 2 children, Cloquet.
Dahlin, Nels, Cloquet.
Davidson, H. J., Cloquet.
Derosiers and 3 girls.
Doddridge, Mrs. Charles and 6 children.
Dodge, Charles, Cloquet.
Dewitt, Mrs. Charles and 2 children, Brookston.
Doro, Mrs., 2705 Railroad street.
Dunham and child, Mrs.
Dennett, Miss and 4 cousins.
Derusha, Mrs. Alex. and 4 children, Cloquet.
Draher, Henry C., Cloquet.
Dryka, J. A., Hunter's Park.
Dalyea, Mr., Cloquet.
Dalyea, Robert, wife and 6 children, Cloquet.
Denny, Wm., and 2 children and 4 grandchildren, Cloquet.
Derouche, Alex., wife and 1 child, Cloquet.
Derusha, Geo., wife and 5 children, Cloquet.
Dahlert, Mrs. Wm. and 3 children, Cloquet.
Donald, wife and 3 children, Cloquet.
Dolan, Mrs. W. G., and children, Cloquet.

Early, Mrs., Cloquet.
Elava, Joe, wife and 3 children, Cloquet.
England, Mrs. and 3 children, Cloquet.
Erickson, Louis, Cloquet.
Edmont, Ray, 3 children, Cloquet.
Egeria, August, Munger.
Ellison, Mrs. M., 5515 London road.
Elfes, O. B., wife and 1 child, Cloquet.
England, Morris, wife, and 5 children, Cloquet.
Engman, Mrs. Minnie and 2 children, Grand Lake.
Engusath, John and child, Morningside Park.
Erickson, Albert and 2 children, Woodland.
Erickson, Albert, wife and 3 children, Hobart street.
Erickson, Alf., Five Corners.
Erickson, J. A., wife and 2 children, Jackson school.
Erickson, Mrs. John, Arnold.
Erickson, Mrs. J. K., Arnold.
Erickson, Hazel, Arnold.
Erickson, Mary.
Ewing, E. J., wife and daughter, 5732 East Superior street.

Fabner, Mr. and Mrs., and 1 child, Cloquet.
Fladell, wife and granddaughter, Cloquet.
Fairbanks, C. O., wife and baby, 5207 G (Jinetta) street.
Faro, Mrs., and 6 children, Woodland.
Fife, Mrs. John, and 2 daughters, Arnold.
Findley, J. J.
Finn, Mrs. W. J., and 8 children, 421

5732 East Superior street.
Heglund, O. N., Rice Lake.
Hudberg, Edw., Cloquet.
Hutchins, Mrs. A. F. and two children, Brookston.
Horning, Mrs. and child, Jackson school.
Harmings, Lars.
Harleck, Vincent and Ann, Arnold.
Heath, Mrs.
Halbert, Mrs. F., Cloquet.
Hickey, R. E. and wife, Proctor.
Hahn, C. F., Woodland.
Hammond, Mrs. Lizzie, 5425 Oakland street.
Hurad, Mrs. Joe and six children, Cloquet.
Hughes, Mrs. George and two children, Cloquet.
Hockert, Mrs. F., Cloquet.
Henricksen, Henry and wife, Cloquet.
Howard, Margaret E., Cloquet.
Homer, four children, Cloquet.
Hulstand, George, wife, boy and mother-in-law, Cloquet.
Holmes, John (alone), Cloquet.
Hari, Mrs., one child, Sawyer.
Hayne, Eva, and child, Cloquet.
Hedberg, Gust, wife and three children, Cloquet.
Hedechristien, Mrs., Cloquet.
Henning, Alver and wife, Arnold.
Henrickson, L., wife and four children, Cloquet.
Hilon, A. and wife, and eight children, Cloquet.
Harning, Lars, Cloquet.
Heasley, F. P., wife and daughter, Cloquet.

Isaacson, Lempi, Cloquet.
Ingelson, Mrs., and two children, Exeter Farms.
Johnson, wife and two children, Cloquet.
Johnson, Elmer, wife and son, Adolph.
Johnson, Frank, 6005 London road.
Johnson, Mrs. Ida B., Exeter Farms.
Johnson, Gustave, wife and children, Cloquet.
Johnson, wife and daughter, Cloquet.
Johnson, Gust A., wife and daughter, Cloquet.
Johnson, G. A.
Johnson, Jacob, Exeter Farms.
Johnson, John C., Lakeside.
Johnson, Mrs. Joe, and four children, Zebulon.
Jansen, Mrs. John, 310 East Superior street.
Janette, Mrs. I., Daniel and Isaac, Harney.
Janette, Emil, wife and child, Harney.
Johnson, Mrs. Marie, and four children, 42925 East Oneida street.
Johnson, Marvin.
Johnson, Zella M., Cloquet.
Joseph, Sam, wife and three children.
Jorson, S. E., and family.
James, (Jammes) Mrs., and daughter, Hermantown.
Jahn, Mrs., girl and small boy.
Jahmia (Jamia), Mr. and Mrs., 1930 North Sixteenth avenue west.
Jacobs, Rose, Park Point.
Juntte, Mrs. Emil and baby, Cloquet.
Juntinen, Mamie, Cloquet.
Johnson, Walt, and seven children, Cloquet.
Jolet, Mrs., and two children, Cloquet.
Joseph, Sam, wife and five children, Cloquet.
Jubey, wife and five children, Cloquet.
Jeroux, Mr., Cloquet.
Johnson, Mamie, Cloquet.
Johnson, Jacob and two children, Exeter Farms.
Johnson, Mrs. Ida and F. P., Exeter Farms.
Johnston, A. W., and two children, 4902 Pitt street east.
Johnson, Mrs. A. John and two children, 5127 Colorado street.
Johnson, Mrs., Adolph.
Johnson, Arthur N., 4925 Oneida street.
Johnson, Mrs. Carl, mother, sister, five children, Brookston.
Johnson, Christ, wife and two children, 4605 Cook street.
Johnson, Charles.

Laundesten, Mrs. and child and mother, 5125 Tioga street.
Larsen, Mrs. Carl, Brookston.
Larsen, C. T., wife and daughter, Brookston.
Larson, Joe.
Larson, Oliver and baby, Brookston.
Larson, William, Arnold.
Lattamus, Gust, Cloquet.
Laundra, Mrs., Morningside park.
Lavasseur, Alphouse, Cloquet.
Lawson, Ole, Jackson school.
Leendeen.
Le Grange, George D., Sixty-fourth avenue east.
Lekowski, Mrs. Sylvester, and Sophia.
Leslie, Victor, three children, Hermantown.
Levassey, Alphonse, wife and four children, Cloquet.
Le May, Vernon, 4528 "J" street.
Lewis, Mrs. Mary, 22 North Palmetto street.
Lewis, Ronald, Palmetto street.
Lindblom, C. J., and two children, 4832 Wyoming street.
Lindblom, C. J., 4832 Wyoming street.
Linemin, Mr. and Mrs. and one child, Lakeside.
Longlen, Benjamin, Woodland.
Lohenau, Louis, Mrs. and daughter, 4521 Dodge street.
Lonson, Anna, Brookston.
Lontin, Ben.
Loons, Louis, Cloquet.
Lowering, Mrs. (Lovering), 5129 Woodland.
Lowri, Joe, Cloquet.
Lowry, Joe, Woodland.
Luezak, Pauline, Hermantown.
Lumppio, Alfred, wife and four children, Cloquet.
Lundberg, Mrs. Mary, husband, six children, Adolph.
Lynch, Helen, Cloquet.
Lynch, Mrs. William and three children.

McMillan, C. T., Cloquet.
McKinnen, Mrs. Frances and daughter, Cloquet.
Mathewson, Mrs. Walter and two boys, 4919 Dodge.
Myrmel, John, Cloquet.
McLaren, Mr. and Mrs., Oneida street
McDonald, Mr. and Mrs. R. A., 227 Faribault.
McDonald, R. A. and daughter and Mrs., Woodland.
MacDowell, Mrs. Lakeside.
McDonald, Mrs. James R., three children, Cloquet.
McTague, John, Cloquet.
MacDowell, Mrs., Lakeside.
McCulloch, Andy, Cloquet.
MacDowell, Mrs., Lakeside.
McCamus, Rowe and wife and four children, Brookston.
McCormick, A., 6815 London road.
McNutt, Mina.
McGillivary, John.
McCubbin, Robert, wife and two children.
McCleod, Hugh, wife and five children, Cloquet.
McElroy, Mrs., Cloquet.
McCorson, Mr. and Mrs. and granddaughter, Greysolon Farms.
McCubry, Albert, wife and child, Cloquet.
Martin, Henry, wife and child, Arnold.
Marcilmak, Francis, two children, Woodland.
Manson, Mrs. James, two children, 5110 Kingston street.
Mittinen, John and wife, and two children, 4812 E. Oneida.
Malzac, Mrs. and two children, Colbyville, Minn.
Mason, Mrs. John and three children, 4009 West First street.
Mettner, Mrs. and child.
Miller, George, Maple Grove road, West Duluth.
Murphy, Clarence (little boy).
Mathewson, Mrs., and two boys.
Materson and two daughters, Woodland.
Meiking, Andrew, wife and three children, Cloquet.
Mickelson, Andrew, wife and daughter, Cloquet.
Moen, H. and three children, Cloquet.
Mixwell, H. W., Cloquet.
Mixsell, Mrs. H. W., Cloquet.

(missing) 494 Palmetto Heights.
Peterson, Peter, Homecroft Park.
Peterson, Emma, Forty-seventh avenue east.
Paakari, Mrs. August and baby, Kettle River.
Pangburn, Mrs. Josephine and one child.
Palmer, Mrs. and two children.
Pelts, Frank and wife, three children.
Pommerville, Vim, Spring Garden.
Peterson, Barney, wife, sister and two children, (at Mrs. Turrish's).
Peterson, Charles, daughter and son, Fiftieth avenue east and Oakly.
Pero, Mrs. Joe and three children, 4427 Oneida street.
Pollock, Mrs. Robert and two children, 5321 Avondale street.
Perrott, Mrs., Duluth Heights.
Price, wife and eight children, Cloquet.
Poirer, Paul and four children, Cloquet.
Pitt, Mrs. and one child, Cloquet.
Pantser, Ed, wife and five children, Cloquet.

Quence, Mrs., Cloquet.
Quze, Mr. and one child, Cloquet.

Roses, John, wife and one child, Cloquet.
Roses, Theodore, wife and four children, Cloquet.
Rock, Mrs. E. and Paul, Brookston.
Roger, Walter, wife and four children, Cloquet.
Roger, Ed, and wife, Cloquet.
Roberts, C. L., and daughter, Olive, and wife, Cloquet.
Roy, Vera, Cloquet.
Roy, Mrs. Mary, Cloquet.
Roses, Bert, wife and three children, Cloquet.
Rosenthal, C., wife and three children, Cloquet.
Rayone, Joe, wife and one child, Cloquet.
Risemowovitch, Joseph, wife and four children, Cloquet.
Ridlington, Dan, and three children, Cloquet.
Richey, Mr. and Mrs., Cloquet.
Rowe, Mrs. B. A. and Mrs. N., 2105 Colorado avenue.
Reight, Mr. and Mrs. Raymond C., Greysolon Farms.
Running, Mrs. Marie Signa, 5325 East Glendale street.
Rancourt, William, Cloquet.
Rush, Mrs. D. D. and daughter, 145 West Anoka street.
Rumming, Mrs. and Miss, Lakeside.
Romberg, Mrs. John and five children, Forty-seventh avenue east.
Roche, Mrs. E. and Paul, Brookston.
Rush, Woodland.
Rumming, S., 5317 Oakley street.
Rowe, Mrs. Bert and daughter (gone home).
Roberts, E. J., Cloquet.
Robison, Mrs. Agnes (gone to Park Point).
Randell, R. O., Cloquet.
Robideau, Mrs. Frank.
Ranberg, Mrs. Johnson, five children (no residence given).
Rappanen, Ina Mrs., Kettle River.

Schreider, R. J., wife and 4 children, Homecroft, Calvary road.
Sabroski, John, wife and 4 children, 5106 Nomgar street.
Stranding, Mrs. Emil and 2 children, 5211 Jenette street.
Segal, Mr. and Mrs., and 8 children.
Silvers, Mr. John T.
Schlines.
Samuelson, Mrs., and 2 children.
Segal, Mr. and Mrs. Oscar, and 7 children, Woodland.
Segal, Laura.
Sindquist, Mrs. J., Calvary road.
Stennes, Olaf, St. James' orphanage.
Swanson, August, Box 38, Canosia, R. F. D. 1.
Scullien, Mrs., Brookland dairy, Exeter Farms.
Strabrodt, Clarence, Herman and little girl.
Shomble, Evelyn, Hermantown.
Smith, Mrs., Lakeside.
Stephen, Fred, Gnesen road.
Schiedmeyer, Louis, wife, 2 children

Trader, John.
Tague, Mrs., Hermantown.
Titus, John, wife and six children, Cloquet.
Throen, Mrs. L., Cloquet.
Thompson, Mrs. A. H., Cloquet.
Toreson, Chris, Exeter Farms.
Twadt, John, wife and children, Cloquet.
Turner, Steve, wife and son, Cloquet.
Trudell, Mr. and Mrs. and two children, Cloquet.

Upton, Mrs. Harry, Beatrice, Violet and Florence, Harry, William and Victor, Arnold.
Upton, Harry, Woodland.
Ullman, daughter, Bertha, Cloquet.

Vickstrom, Mrs., 810 North Twenty-first avenue west.
Vera, Roy, Cloquet.
Vickstrom, Mrs. Angie.

Walker, H. H., and wife, Cloquet.
Walquist, Richard, and wife, Crosley Park.
Wentz, Mrs. Cora, and two grandchildren, Cloquet.
Wesling, Oscar, wife and three children, Cloquet.
Westman, Eleanor, and granddaughter, 116 West Palmetto.
Whittaker, Carrie and Louis, Brookston.
Wahlin, Nels and wife, gone to A. B. Wolvin's.
Welling and four children, Exeter Farms (1515 East First street).
Wilcox, W. P., wife and child, Homecroft Park.
Whittmore, Mr. and Mrs., and two children, Cloquet.
Warri, Walt, Sawyer.
Welsh, Mrs., Cloquet.
Webritt, Thomas, wife and children, Cloquet.
Watt, wife and one child, Cloquet.
Wurek, Miss, Cloquet.
Woodmaid, Laura, taken to Y. W. C. A., room 410.
Warner, Carlton, Woodland.
Weston, Fannie, Cloquet.
Whitebird, Mrs. Frank, Cloquet.
Whitebird, Mrs. Anna, Cloquet (at courthouse).
Wilcox, William, wife and three children, Cloquet (at courthouse).
Whihelm, Leona, Pike Lake (at courthouse).
Winship, Mrs., Cloquet (at Spalding).
Wall, John, Shaw (at Brunswick hotel).
White, Mrs. Charles, and two boys, Road 4, City Box 54.
Walson, Anton, two miles from Jean Duluth farm.
Wakefield, Mrs. E., Jr.
Walquist, Richard, and wife.
Wicklund, Mrs. Oscar, and baby, 5131 Colorado street.
Whaprinba, Mrs., and daughter, 4917 Jay street.
Wilson, Mrs. Erick, and five children, Brookston (Morrisey's).
Wagner, Mrs. G. E., and two children, Nebagamon.
Winters, James, and wife, at Fourth avenue east and Fourth street.
Wilson, Mrs. John, and son, Rice Lake.
White, Gleen, La Crosse (Sixty-fourth avenue east).
Webb, Mr., Woodland (at Kitchi Gammi club).
Wise, Mrs. Louis, and four children, Cloquet (at 1401 E. Ninth street).
Wait, Mrs., Lakeside (taken to Y. W. C. A.).
Walkia, Thomas, wife and child, Cloquet.
Westine, Mrs. Charles, and three children, Cloquet.

Young, William, wife and one child, Cloquet.

Zazidski, three children, Cloquet.
Zala, Felix, and four children, Cloquet.
Zebitt, Mrs., Cloquet.
Zevatt, Mr., and wife.
Ziloski, Sylvester, wife and two children, Cloquet.
Ziehl, Mrs. Rose, Sixtieth avenue east.

This alphabetized list of fire survivors appeared in The Duluth Herald *on October 14, 1918.*

Carlton County Vidette.

VOLUME NO. XXXI. THE CARLTON COUNTY VIDETTE, CARLTON, CARLTON COUNTY, MINNESOTA. FRIDAY, OCTOBER 18, 1918. NUMBER 46.

AWFULLEST FIRE HORROR IN STATE'S HISTORY!
Probably 900 Lives Gone! Property Loss Also Terrible!

City of Cloquet Wiped Out By a Seething Holocaust With a Loss of Probably Twenty Million Dollars!

---oOo---

Moose Lake and Kettle River, 24 Other Towns Wiped Out With Hundreds Of Lives Lost!

---oOo---

Beggering description was the awful catastrophe which visited this section, the hurricane of flame and burning leaves and smoke which swept at a 60 or 70 mile speed though the forests, cities and towns of this district last Saturday afternoon and night, carrying death and devastation in its hell-like path!

INSURANCE NOTICE!

Adjusters for Hartford Fire Insurance Company are on the ground. Claimants please address or communicate with Agent C. P. Osburn, either at Cloquet or Sellwood Building Duluth.

SPECIAL NOTICE TO FARMERS

The Carlton county authorities urge every farmer not to sell their stock. Unprincipled buyers have been going through the county buying up all stock obtainable at prices much under their value, explaining to the owners that with no feed in the county they will all be lost anyway. The authorities are hurrying hay and supplies here as rapidly as can be done, and expect in a few days to have enough feed here to save all stock. Every farmer should make application to the relief committee at their own town or notify the county auditor.

left. Most of the Cloquet lumber yards on Dunlap Island are saved, and most of everything north of the Great Northern Railroad tracks, but everything south of the tracks is completely swept clean—even the ashes mostly blown away by the terrific gale. Cloquet has a bunch of energetic, determined business men—some of the biggest men, mentally and financially, in the United States, and when they set out to accomplish an object nothing in the power of humanity can stop them. And these men, with set teeth, cheerful dispositions, in the face of having just lost millions of dollars, say, "You bet, we will build up Cloquet. Many of our faithful boys, who have worked with us for years, say they will be back with us just as soon as we can find a place for them to live, and we will find it." Before the smoke had cleared away meetings of the prominent men had been held at Carlton, and plans formulated for immediate erection of temporary quarters for their men, and on Monday morning, Senator Vibert, under direction of prominent men of the city,

LODGES HASTEN TO RELIEVE THEIR MEMBERS

The local lodges came to the relief of their members in splendid shape.
Dr. Edward H. Hass, state commander of Maccabees was in Carlton and Cloquet, Wednesday ready to provide relief to members of that organization.
Edward F. Burns, state deputy of the M. W. A., and B. A. Erickson, of Duluth, were in Carlton and Cloquet Wednesday organizing relief for their members. They had made provisions for a portable sawmill at Hermantown, for the farmers. The Odd Fellows and Masons have also taken quick steps to relieve needy members.
Notice to members of the Scandinavian-American Fraternity and the Order of Sons of Norway.
The supreme lodge of the Scandinavian-American Fraternity and also the grand lodge of the Order of Sons of Norway, has announced that they wish to aid members of the local lodges "Sulitjelma" of A. S. E., and "Heimsyn" of S. of N., located at Cloquet, or other places in the burnt district of this county, or members belonging to other lodges of the respective orders and prior to the fire residing in this county.
Both said orders have appointed Julius B. Baumann, Register of Deeds at Carlton, Minn. All in need will please notify him at once. Call in per-

OCTOBER DRAFT CALL IS CANCELLED NOW

The local draft board, in view of the big calamity, made heroic efforts to get our county draft call for October cancelled. On Thursday they got word from Adj. Gen. Rhinow notifying them that the call has been cancelled for thirty days. This is official notice to the boys who were to go, that they do not need to go for thirty days, at least.

SAVE M'GREGOR AFTER BIG FIGHT

On Thursday Afternoon Town Was Circled By Flames.

Brainerd, Minn., Oct. 15.—(Special to The Herald.)—The fire around Cromwell is checked according to F. C. Shrafklin, Brainerd man, who motored through that district Thursday.
A hard fight was made at McGregor and the town was saved.
At 9:30 a. m. there were no fires there and at 4 in the afternoon fires were on all sides of McGregor.
Forty-two Grey Eagle Home Guards left home that night and passed through Brainerd on their way to Kimberly, which is headquarters for assembling guards.

INSURANCE COMPANIES ESTABLISH HEADQUARTERS

On October 19, 1918, the Carlton County Vidette *published many stories about the fires. Since accurate information was not yet available, many of the newspaper articles that were written soon after the fire, exaggerated the numbers of people who had died.*

Fire Storm: The Great Fires of 1918

CHAPTER FOUR

THE DULUTH FIRES

Duluth Is Threatened by the Fire

The City of Duluth was threatened by the fire that had its main source at Milepost 62 near Brookston and burned over twenty-nine miles to the eastern edge of Duluth. The fire was reported to have jumped to the east bank of the St. Louis River south of Brookston shortly after 4:00 p.m. Meanwhile a gravel train on the Duluth, Missabe and Northern tracks, had started fires along the roadbed between Culver and Alborn about 2:00 p.m. Although railroad workers and local people attempted to put out the fires there and at Stony Brook Road, the fires quickly got out of control all along the tracks and began burning farms. Other smaller fires also joined with the Milepost 62 fire to create a long fire front that was moving at fifteen to twenty miles per hour with winds that gusted from eighty to ninety miles an hour.[65]

The rural areas north and west of Duluth were burned. This photo shows the empty mailbox of a farm that was burned and is still smoldering.

Photo by Hugh McKenzie from the collection of CCHS

The strong winds blew the fire to the east and southeast and created a dangerous situation for the communities north and west of Duluth. A large farming community was badly overrun by the fire south of the Swan Lake Road. By late afternoon the Grand Lake, Saginaw, and Twig areas were also burning. The *Duluth News Tribune* of October 14 reported that the communities of Adolph, Munger, Five Corners, Harney, Munger, and Pine Hill had all been destroyed.

Pike Lake

Pike Lake was a popular place for boating, swimming, and having picnics. On October 12th, many people from Duluth had gone to Pike Lake to spend the day or the weekend at summer homes and cottages there. As the fire came closer to the lake, some people went back to Duluth. Others stayed and were caught by the fire. A number of people lost their lives as they tried to outrun the fire in automobiles and, in the smoke and confusion, there was a pileup of cars on the Pike Lake Road.

Automobiles piled up along the roads and in ditches north of Duluth as people tried to flee from the flames. Many lives were lost in this area.

Photos by Hugh McKenzie from the collection of CCHS

Some people tried to escape the fire by going out on Pike Lake in their boats. The strong winds created waves that overturned the boats and several families were drowned. A number of well-known Duluthians who had been celebrating a birthday lost their lives when their boat capsized (tipped over) and they drowned in the cold waters of the lake.

Although the loss of life was heavy (as many as 100 people) in the Pike Lake area, many lives were saved by courageous people who drove their automobiles from Duluth into the burning areas to rescue people. The Duluth newspaper reported, "The response of Duluth autoists in giving their cars and personal services during the fire has been remarkable, and hundreds of lives were saved by the timely and efficient work of these car owners, who drove fearlessly in the face of fire over dangerous roads."[66]

Outlying Areas of Duluth

Other outlying areas of Duluth suffered much damage and loss of lives. Almost all of the prosperous dairy farms of Hermantown were at least partially burned and much livestock was lost. It was difficult to feed the cattle that survived because most of the haystacks were burned. Only about six of the forty-seven buildings in Maple Grove survived, but nearby Proctor suffered no damage and was able to take in about 1,200 refugees.[67]

A well-known landmark was burned out. A farmer's cart and a pig can been seen on the road.

Photo by Hugh McKenzie from the collection of CCHS

Military units were called into action to help fight fire and to help with the relief efforts after the fire. The Fourth Regiment of the National Guard was driven to Hermantown by the Minnesota Motor Corps (an adjunct of the Minnesota Home Guard) to fight the fire. They saved both lives and property there. The Third and Seventh Battalions of the Home Guard helped to defend Woodland from the flames. Members of the Third Battalion and volunteers with automobiles evacuated patients at the Nopeming Sanatorium (county run tuberculosis hospital). The patients, including forty children and babies, were taken to the Irving Junior High School and Denfeld High School by over fifty automobiles. The Bridgeman-Russell Company supplied 100 quarts of milk and a case of eggs for the children during the night. Nopeming did not burn and the patients returned there within a day or so.

Automobiles were lined up ready to evacuate the children who lived at the St. James orphanage at the end of the Woodland trolley car line. Although the fire burned on both sides of the driveway leading to the building, the orphanage did not burn and the children were finally put to bed around 10:30 p.m. About twenty mothers and children from Arnold found a safe place there after their own homes were destroyed.

The fire burned into the neighborhoods of Lakewood, Lester Park, and Lakeside where the flames reached all the way to Lake Superior in some places. Property losses were reported in the Knife River Valley including the Tettegoucha clubhouse on the Gooseberry River which was a hunting lodge owned by Duluth men. The village of Two Harbors was saved by a wind blowing off Lake Superior, although buildings burned in nearby Larsmont and Waldo. A small settlement at Lax Lake was destroyed and some residents fled to Beaver Bay.[68]

Thomas Gray was alone on the farm in Lakewood when the fire came. He wrapped his feet in wet newspapers and his body in wet blankets. Then he lay down in the French River. "The fire came through, but missed Mr. Gray and the buildings! It burned the wooden handles off the farm implements that had been left so hurriedly in a field of freshly plowed soil."[69]

Adrian Heino wrote about his experiences near Lake Superior in Duluth Township:

> The fire of 1918 was a traumatic experience. Smoke was everywhere, and the sun was a brilliant red. Early in the day, the Alex Johnsons brought their children to our house, feeling they were, in some measure, safer with us because of the wide clearing around the farm. During the night, with the fires only one-half mile away, a shift in the wind spared our farm, but most of the homes on the Ryan Road were destroyed.[70]

Duluth is Saved

Crews of volunteers, military troops, and the Duluth Fire Department worked into the night putting out spot fires along the top of the Duluth hills. But some structures well into the city were burned— Northland Country Club, the Alger-Smith Lumber Company on Rice's Point, and the Interstate bridge connecting Duluth and Superior were all or partly destroyed.

Strong winds of about fifty to sixty miles per hour blew in Duluth from about 4:00 p.m. to 9:00 p.m. The winds decreased in speed to around forty miles per hour from 9:00 p.m. until about 2:00 a.m. They died down after that and the city was saved. If the winds had not changed and the fire had come into the city, it would have been a terrible tragedy. The large number of people in the city could not have left town—it was surrounded by fire and the roads were blocked. The water of Lake Superior was too cold to survive in for any period of time and the waves on the Lake were too high for boats to be launched.[71]

Duluthians explore the burned out ruins of the Northland Country Club located in the Lakeside neighborhood of Duluth.

Photo by Hugh McKenzie from the collection of CCHS

Grateful Duluthians entered into the relief efforts at once and opened their homes, civic buildings, and churches to the refugees providing food, clothing, and medical care. News headlines tell the story—

Charities Take Care of Scores

**Quick Assistance Given Fire Victims—
Y.M.C.A. and Y.W.C.A. do Part**

Business Houses Provide Clothing and Food for Destitute

**Churches Open to Refugees,
Many Fire Sufferers Find Food and Shelter in Them**

**Red Cross, Physicians and Many Others
Perform Efficient Service.**

Moose Lake is one of the oldest towns in Carlton County. The top photo is an early "bird's eye" view showing Moosehead Lake and the buildings of the town. The lower photo was taken shortly before the fire and shows a bustling street scene with substantial buildings and telephone lines.

Photos from the collection of CCHS

CHAPTER FIVE

ISLANDS OF FLAMES

The Moose Lake/Kettle River Fire Areas

The stories of the fires in southern Carlton County and the surrounding region are ones of terrible destruction of property and loss of lives. Farms, schools, churches, and whole towns including Automba, Lawler, Kettle River, and Moose Lake were destroyed. Many people and countless wild and domestic (farm) animals died.

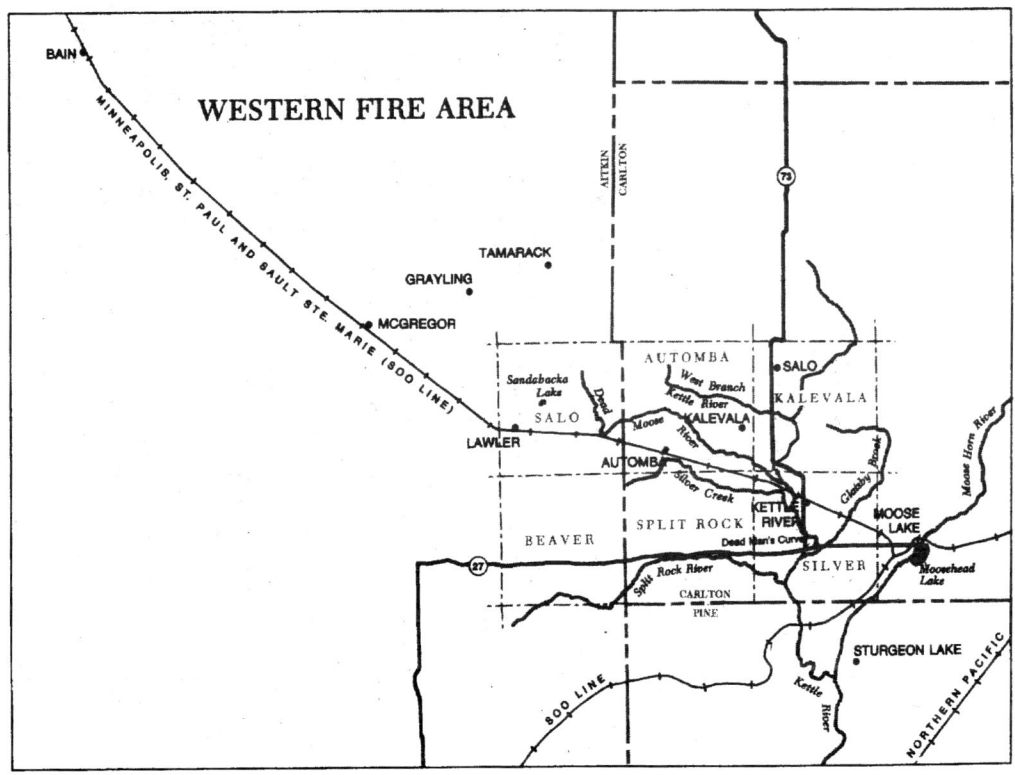

This map of the Western Fire Area shows the towns of Automba, Kettle River, and Moose Lake that were destroyed by the fire. Dead Man's Curve is just south of Kettle River and west of Moose Lake.

Map reproduced from Fires of Autumn, Minnesota Historical Society Press

There were five major fires in this region extending into Carlton, Aitkin, and Pine Counties. The largest of these was the Moose Lake/Kettle River Fire. It burned an area between McGregor and Tamarack in the northwest to just beyond Moose Lake and Sturgeon Lake in the southeast. At the center of this fire was the Soo Line tracks. This fire spread from Lawler to Automba, Kettle River, and Moose Lake along the tracks. The fire stretched as far as thirty-one miles wide and fourteen miles long.

The second largest fire was farther northwest along the Soo Line tracks in Aitkin County. The small community of Bain was at the heart of this fire. The third largest fire spread from the Willow River area, along the Northern Pacific tracks, to Bruno, and then along the Great Northern tracks to the edges of Cloverton. Two other sizable fires ignited—one at White Pine, and another at Arthyde, towns which were located south of Moose Lake. Other, smaller fires burned in the region as well.

Not only did the three major railroad tracks of the Soo Lines, the Great Northern, and the Northern Pacific crisscross the region, they determined the fire areas. Most people believed the railroad companies were mainly responsible for the cause of the fires.[72]

Tamarack

On October 4th George Brand, a Northern Pacific fire patrolman, spotted a fire burning on the north side of the tracks between Grayling and Tamarack. By October 9th the fire had crossed the track. A Northern Pacific section crew (a team of railroad men) was sent to fight the fire. They were able to stop the fire from reaching Tamarack but were unable to put it out. When the high winds and low relative humidity set in on October 12th, the fires flared up. Workers from the Nelson Sawmill were sent home early in the day to make firebreaks with their plows. They worked from 1:00 p.m. until 3:00 a.m. the next morning to fight the fire.

Meanwhile Mrs. Marcus Nelson, owner of the Nelson sawmill, telegraphed Minnesota Governor Burnquist for help. He responded by sending Home Guard troops from Aitkin to help fight the fire. By afternoon they had arrived. Orvis Nelson recalled that "their presence that night undoubtedly saved the town."[73]

To escape the fire in Tamarack most of the people took one of the two Northern Pacific relief trains that were sent to pick up the fire survivors. By 6:00 p.m. two of the cars on one of the trains caught on fire. The burning cars were quickly broken loose from the train. The rest of the train made its way back to Carlton. In the meantime, the second train made trips between Cromwell and Tamarack throughout the night and the next day picking up fire survivors. Many farmers and their families who lived in these rural areas simply fled to a freshly plowed field or clearing.

Lawler

On October 12 another serious railroad fire started at Milepost 263 along the Soo Line tracks near Lawler. The sixty to one hundred miles per hour winds hurled sparks from the train causing the bog fires to flare up and burn into the woods.

The high winds drove the fire with such speed and force that farmers found themselves in the midst of the blaze without any warning. Ditching the knocked over trees, flaming boards, and hurling haystacks many farmers fled to an open field. Aili Rosbacka Field later recalled her experience in a plowed field:

> Father and I shielded both Mother and my brother, Uno, from the fire. We had to "dig in" with our faces into the ground to prevent suffocation. My elbow, arm, and knee were burned while trying to cover other members of the family. We often think how courageously our neighbor, Mrs. Abel Salo, saved her children and herself on a plowed field. (Mr. Salo was away at work.)[74]

Other farmers fled to streams or lakes. Among them was Miriam Sanda Shilston who remembered her mother's brave actions that night:

> My mother refused to leave her home, feeling that we had the best chance of survival near the water. It was her forethought and calmness that saved all of our lives. It was in the safety of the boats where 17 children—we five and the children of our neighbors...were herded...I can still remember the chilly, frightening night and the pails of cold water that were thrown over us whenever the flames from across the lake occasionally threatened to set fire to our clothes.[75]

Still others sought shelter in their root cellars. For Carl Koivunen, "Mama" Koivunen, and two others this resulted in death by suffocation. They were the only people in Salo Township who lost their lives.[76]

Many people from the town caught a Soo relief train that had been sent from Riverton. C.A. Hanna recalls, "[the depot] burst into flames and exploded." Everything in town burned except for the school, a hotel, the telephone office, and Spicola Brothers' store.[77]

Flames in Automba

The fire sped onward in a southeasterly direction along the Soo Line Tracks and the Dead Moose River towards Automba. On October 12th the fire entered the lumber yards of Charles Jokimaki's sawmill on the Dead Moose River around 3:30 p.m. Charles Jokimaki's partner, William Maki, had this to say:

> That Saturday, most of the men from the surrounding area had tried most of the day to get the fire under control, but it slowly inched its way toward Automba. In the afternoon the wind started to blow harder and harder until finally we realized the situation was hopeless. Some people started to leave right away, but most did not become alarmed or start to flee until the lumber yards caught fire. The intense heat and flying, burning boards from the yards turned the little town of Automba into an island of flames in a matter of minutes.[78]

The small logging town of Aubomba lies in ruins after the fire passed through the town. Tents are being used as temporary shelters by the fire survivors. The fire came so quickly, that residents often saved only the clothes they were wearing.

Photo by T. J. Horton, Minnesota Forest Service, published in American Foresty

Charles Jokimaki and his wife fled by automobile heading south towards Split Rock. Before long his automobile caught on fire. They fled to an open field and stayed there until the fire passed over.

Meanwhile on the north side of Automba the escape for some members of the William Jokimaki family ended in tragedy. Shortly after 4:00 p.m. one million board feet of lumber in Jacobson's sawmill caught on fire. Their flaming boards landed on a haystack on the nearby William Jokimaki farm. Aina Jokimaki Johnson recalls her family fleeing to a nearby swamp where they got separated:

> The terrifying inferno was over and above and all around us...We were all soon separated. [I] somehow got off the trail directly into the midst of burning saw logs. Running and jumping over these burning logs, I was desperately seeking my way home. Imagine yourself, a terrified young girl in shock...I was wearing stockings and high top shoes, but although none of my clothes burned, my feet actually baked inside my shoes and stockings. I still have scars to remind me of that night. I will have them to my dying day.[79]

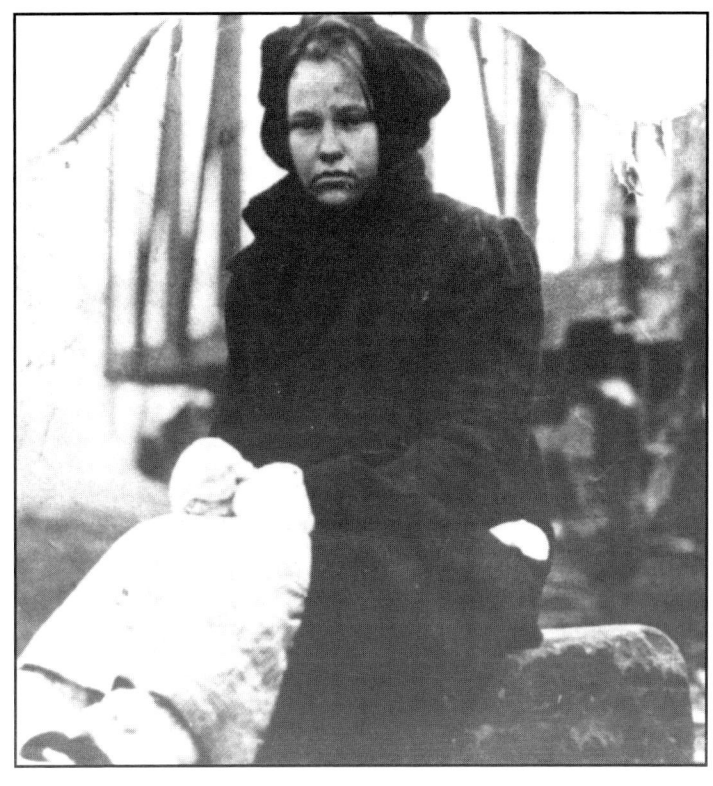

Sixteen year old Aina Jokimaki was badly burned on her hands and legs in the fire. Her mother and six brothers and sisters all died in the blaze.

Photo by William Bull from the collection of CCHS

That evening Aina found her father, severely burned, but alive by a stream. She later learned that her mother, Suoma, as well as her six brothers and sisters; one cousin; and neighbors had lost their lives in the fire.

What was left of Automba, after the fire? This town of about 350 people was completed destroyed. Twenty-three residents had been killed as they attempted to escape.

Kettle River Burns

A fire that had started along the Soo Line tracks on September 30th burned toward farms close to Kettle River. By October 12th many men from the area had come to fight the fire and work on a firebreak. By 5:00 p.m. the fire was burning out of control and the men scattered to try to save their families and farms. Between fifteen and twenty firefighters were trapped in the blaze and died near Highway 73.

By 6:00 p.m. the fire was entering Kettle River and people were looking for some way of escaping the burning town. All afternoon a sixteen year old telephone operator for the Kettle River Telephone Exchange, Aili Leppa Nikkila, was "swamped with calls from the residents pleading for assistance." She recalled, "soon the entire neighborhood was in panic and confusion. The sky was overcast and filled with smoke and flying debris and flames."[80]

A Soo Line relief train made up of an engine, tender, and caboose reached Kettle River from Moose Lake around 6:00 p.m. Because of the fire it could not travel any further west and began picking up people at the train station, the section house, and the railroad crossing. It was forced to back up all the way to Moose Lake packed with frightened men, women, and children.[81]

Still others like the Soboleski family from Kettle River sought shelter in wells:

> The well was shallow and had gone dry a while back. It was only four feet square at the opening, shored by logs all the way down to the bottom, eleven feet away. Only people are going to fit down there, nothing else. The makeshift ladder fit flush to the top and would have to hold 17 people unless the younger ones could squeeze around the bottom. A bale of straw was thrown down the hole and they began to file down, Elizabeth first with baby Anton. She would find a comfort of sorts being able to sit while the others would withstand the ordeal on their feet.[82]

The Soboleski's were fortunate as many who chose the wells and root cellars for their place of refuge became victims of asphyxiation (death resulting from lack of oxygen). Many people went into root cellars (an outdoor room typically underground with a sod roof and used to store canned and fresh vegetables) to find shelter.

Betty Bergman Erickson had this to say of her night spent in the root cellar:

> The roothouse was cool after the heat above. A count of the group was taken. Eight in all. The little group sat down on the edges of the filled potato bins. Even through the thick sod roof they could hear the rumble and the roar of the fire and the wind howling and screaming like a thousand loosed

Fire Storm: The Great Fires of 1918 54

demons. Minutes dragged by like hours. Whenever the trap door was lifted ever so slightly, the thick smoke, heavy with sparks and cinders would roll in. Blankets were spread in the potato bins and the weary gathering lay down to get some rest. [When they awoke in the morning they sat] on the edge of the potato bins and ate bread, butter, and preserved peaches from the rows of cans on the shelves.[83]

People thought the root cellars would be safe and not burn like the wooden houses, but members of several families died in root cellars when the oxygen was used up by the fire. Sixteen children from three families died in one root cellar near Moose Lake. The parents of eight of the children had stayed on the outside trying to keep the flames away from the wooden door.

Several people died in this root cellar near Kettle River.

Photo by Hugh McKenzie from the collection of CCHS

About four miles north of Kettle River, the Kalevala Finnish Evangelical National Lutheran Church did not burn and was later used by the Red Cross and the National Guard. It also became a makeshift hospital to care for influenza patients.

Kettle River was added to the lists of villages completely destroyed by the fire. The burned out bank building was about all that remained in the ruins of the town.

Dead Man's Curve

Many of the people from Kettle River and the surrounding area tried to escape the fire by traveling south on a small dirt road toward

55 Fire Storm: The Great Fires of 1918

Moose Lake. About two miles south of Kettle River the road took a sharp corner. Because of the heavy, dark smoke the drivers couldn't see well and many automobiles missed the corner and piled up. Some tipped over into the ditches and their passengers were thrown out. A number of people walked to the nearby Glaisby Brook and found safety in the water there. But between seventy-five and one hundred people died at Dead Man's Curve, and many were seriously burned.

Members of the National Guard are pictured with wrecked automobiles at Dead Man's Curve south of Kettle River where many people died.

Photo from Forest Fires in Minnesota 1918

Eckman's Corner

Axel Hammerstrom's family had a farm west of Moose Lake about one and one-quarter miles north of the Eckman School. Axel was a student at Barnum High School and had come to the farm for the weekend with his cousin, Jens Freese of Barnum. When the fire came Axel took refuge with the family in a plowed field, but Jens became separated from the group. He was later found with another schoolmate, Erick Holmberg—both burned to death. Jens was the only Barnum victim of the fire.[84]

Over sixty people died near "Eckman's Corner"—many of them at the West Side Church and Eckman School. In spite of the fierce fires in the area the Eckman house was not burned, and as many as one hundred survivors found shelter there during the night. Many of them suffered from serious burns which Dr. F. R. Walters treated when he came there from Moose Lake in the morning.

Moose Lake is Destroyed

A railroad fire less than a mile west of Moose Lake was spotted by Gilbert Buxter during the first week of August. Buxter watched as sparks from the Soo Line passenger train ignited the bog alongside the tracks. For the next two months a section crew fought the fire but was unable to put it out. By October, thirteen fires were burning along a twenty-eight mile stretch of Soo Line tracks west of Moose Lake. State district forest ranger, Perry Swedberg, ordered a crew of up to a hundred men to fight the fires on October 9th.

After 7:00 p.m. on October 12th as the fire burned through Automba and Kettle River, it formed a fire front that extended from Kalevala Township six or seven miles south into Silver Township. The fire was moving at a speed of fifteen to twenty miles per hour and the city of Moose Lake was directly in the path of the fire.

Earlier, two Northern Pacific relief trains had been sent from Hinckley and one from Carlton. The three trains took more than three hundred people from Moose Lake and Sturgeon Lake to safety. But by 7:30 or 8:00 p.m. the fire was in Moose Lake and people were forced to take refuge in the cold waters of Moosehead Lake.

The *Superior Telegram* reported on October 14th:

> The people of Moose Lake were alarmed all Saturday afternoon but from the time the first glow of the flames were seen over the hill to the northwest, until the town was in flames seemed but a few minutes. The wind was so terrific that people were lifted off their feet and blown considerable distances.

The paper went on to describe how people took shelter in the lake:

> It seemed as if great balls of fire were falling from the sky. Moose [head] Lake, the shore of which is just a few blocks from what was the business district, offered the only shelter. Cars loaded with people drove to the lake and were driven right into the water where many of them remain. The water protected the bodies of people but their heads had to be shielded from the brands of fire that were falling by holding wet clothes above. A concrete bridge, with shallow water under it, protected great numbers. Had it not been for the nearby water, no one in Moose Lake, a town of 700 or 800 people, could have hoped to escape death or a fate as bad by being burned and maimed.[85]

Many people escaped the fire and saved their lives by driving their automobiles into Moosehead Lake.

Photo by Olaf Olson from the collection of CCHS

Edith Brattlof (Mrs. Carl Bruno) was a teacher in Moose Lake. She was forced to enter the lake to escape the fire and had this experience, "To protect her head, a man next to Edith took off his heavy sweater, doused it in the water, and covered her with it. Soon afterward, a chicken, flying from the flames that were consuming Moose Lake, flew on Edith's head for refuge."[86]

Mrs. Jack Kohtala was a nurse for Dr. Walters and told this story:

> There were two patients in the hospital at that time. Doctor Walters decided to load them all into his car with some children and make a dash for Sturgeon Lake. He never made it there, though, because the fire had burned across the road by that time and he had to rush back to Moose Lake. With the car starting on fire, the doctor just made it back to the lake, driving right into it with the auto. Although the two patients were very ill, (one had just been on the operating table), they all had to drop into the icy water to keep from burning.[87]

Those who took refuge in the water watched as the city burned and listened to the sound of ammunition exploding in the hardware store. By about 10:00 p.m. it was safe enough to come out of the water and find shelter and warmth.

Almost all of the town of Moose Lake had been destroyed including the telegraph office. Richard Hart, the mayor of Moose Lake, walked the six miles to Sturgeon Lake where he telegraphed Governor J. A. Burnquist to ask for help for the people of Moose Lake and the surrounding area.

Burned out buildings line the main street of Moose Lake after the fire.

Photo from the collection of MHS

The loss of life in this part of the fire area was terrible. The National Guard was sent to look for injured people and to recover the bodies of those who had died. In Moose Lake a mass grave was dug to bury over two hundred people who perished in the fire. It was not even possible to identify many of the victims.

Some of the communities that burned never were rebuilt while others like Moose Lake and Kettle River eventually recovered from the fire. Headlines in the November 8, 1918, *Carlton County Vidette* read,

MOOSE LAKE WILL RISE FROM ASHES

Cars are lined up in front of a makeshift morgue in Moose Lake, ready to take coffins for a mass burial.

Almost 200 victims of the fire were buried on October 15, 1918, in a mass grave in Riverside Cemetery in Moose Lake.

Photos by Olaf Olson from the collection of CCHS

CHAPTER SIX

AFTER THE FIRE

Cloquet Is Destroyed

The morning of October 13th arrived. Many people returned to Cloquet to see what was left. Devastation could be seen everywhere. Gone was the wind that gusted from 65 to 85 miles per hour, gone was the wail of mill sirens and train whistles, gone were the homes, the hospital, and five of the six schools. In its place were blackened hills, dogs howling for masters not there, and remains of home basements.[88]

Cloquet was a scene of desolation the day after the fire.

Photo from the collection of CCHS

But there was good news. Over 8,000 people had been safely evacuated from Cloquet, only four deaths were reported, and much of the industry was saved. Still standing were the two mills of the Cloquet Lumber Company, the Northwest Paper mill (now Sappi), the Johnson-Wentworth Lumber Mill, and the Berst-Forster-Dixfield toothpick factory (now Diamond Brands). Other buildings untouched were the Garfield School and several homes.[89]

The Minnesota Home Guard, Motor Corps, and National Guard

Among the people who were first to inspect the damages of the city was Major Weaver of the Minnesota Home Guard. Seeing that the mills, store safes, and bank vaults remained among the burned and deserted city, he knew the town needed military protection from would-be looters and profiteers (one who makes excessive profits by charging high prices). He immediately went back to Duluth and passed the word on to the National Guard. Meanwhile Minnesota Governor Joseph Burnquist declared the city under martial law.[90]

By 8:30 on Sunday morning the National Guard arrived in Cloquet and set up their headquarters on the east side of Dunlap Island. Among the first things they did was to maintain law and order in the city. They did this by patrolling the town and requiring anyone who wished to return to show some proof of property ownership in town. Typically, the Cloquet residents could get their proof of property ownership or "Title of Deed" by going to the Carlton County Courthouse where these legal papers were kept. The proof of property ownership was a great help in stopping sightseers and souvenir hunters from getting into town.[91]

Besides being the initial agency to protect property, the National Guard was first to give out medical and relief supplies throughout the fire area. In Cloquet they set up a dispensary (place where medicines and first-aid are available) at the Northeastern Hotel on Dunlap Island. Here they treated burned and injured fire survivors. If further treatment was needed at a hospital either they, or the Motor Corps, provided the transportation service.[92]

The National Guardsmen were among the first people to provide relief services in the burned out areas. They are pictured here in front of the tents that served as barracks.

Photo by Fred Levie from the collection of MHS

The National Guard provided many other services. These included building barracks, burying dead animals, building outhouses over sewer manholes, and setting up mess services (feeding stations) for the returning refugees. When fallen trees, charred automobiles, and debris blocked the roads, they cleared them. In some cases they rebuilt roads that collapsed as a result of wooden culverts burning.

They provided search and rescue operations for injured and trapped people and recovered bodies of the dead.[93]

The Motor Corps, a volunteer unit of the Minnesota Home Guard, offered their cars as means to transport the Home Guard throughout the fire disaster area. They played a key role in transporting firefighters, rescuers, and the injured as well as supplies of food, clothing, and medicine to trains.[94]

The Duluth Armory and the Red Cross

The Duluth Armory served as headquarters for the relief efforts. From there the efforts of the National Guard and the Home Guard were directed and the troops mobilized. The Red Cross quickly set up an emergency hospital in the dormitory of the armory and were ready to receive injured people when they arrived by train from the fire areas. Many doctors and nurses volunteered to help care for the injured people and city hotels and stores provided needed supplies, beds, and bedding. Because there was not room for all of the refugees at the armory, the Red Cross arranged for housing in many of Duluth's public buildings.

Refugees and relief workers sort through stacks of donated clothes at the Duluth Armory.

Photo by Hugh McKenzie from the collection of CCHS

National Guard and Home Guard cooks served hot meals to nearly three thousand refugees during the first two days after the fire. The armory also served as a place for refugees who had been separated from their families to register and receive messages. Long lists with the names of refugees and where they had been housed were prepared and published in the newspapers in Duluth and Superior.

People of Carlton, Superior, Duluth and many surrounding small towns such as Proctor, Hinckley, Aitkin, and Sandstone generously provided services and supplies to the fire victims. This could be anything from serving hot meals, providing carloads of clothing, providing medical assistance for the injured, and opening their homes, churches, schools, and halls for shelter. [95]

Fire refugee children receive clothes donated by the St. Paul Winter Carnival. The clothes are being distributed by National Guardsmen.

Photo by St. Paul Dispatch *from the collection of MHS*

The Minnesota Fires Relief Commission

Minnesota Governor Joseph A. Burnquist arrived at the fire stricken areas on Monday, October 14th. Upon seeing the devastation, he immediately created the Minnesota Forest Fires Relief Commission to take over-all responsibility for the relief operations in the fire disaster area. By October 18th the Commission set up their operations in the Duluth Armory gradually replacing the temporary services of the Red Cross, military, and private groups. At first the Commission started with a $300,000 fund and then, in February, received an additional $1,850,000 from the State of Minnesota. The governor also appealed to people in the state to generously donate money to the Commission and people throughout the state responded to the governor's appeal.[96]

The Commission decided to create local committees in each town to better serve their needs. This made it easier for the fire survivors for they could report their losses as well as their needs to a representative on the committee. Relief that they provided to the fire survivors included food, clothing, shoes, and shelter. Food rations (coupons used for free food) were distributed to the survivors so they could buy their own food and not be dependent upon mess services.[97]

How much money, goods, and services the refugees received largely depended upon whether they were a city worker or a country farmer. Unlike most of the city workers who had jobs in the mills for a source of income, the country workers had no immediate source of income. Gone were not only their homes, but also their livestock, feed, farm tools, and equipment. A source of income for them wouldn't occur until next year's harvest in the fall. For this reason the Commission provided more aid to the country workers.[98]

Cloquet Jobs Restored

Miraculously Cloquet still held a future due to the heroic attempts made by a few men who stayed back to fight the fire and save three of the five sawmills. Left standing were the two mills of the Cloquet Lumber Company, and the Johnson-Wentworth Lumber Company.[99]

The question everyone asked was, "Would the mills run again now that the fire had burned so much of the white pine forest?" This answer to the future of Cloquet rested mainly with the decisions made by the three managers of the lumber companies: Rudolph Weyerhaueser of the Northern Lumber Company, Henry Hornby of the Cloquet Lumber Company, and Joseph Wilson of the Johnson-Wentworth Lumber Company. Their decision to ask their employees to come back to work the day after the fire was key to the city's survival.[100]

Rudoph Weyerhaeuser was president of the Northern Lumber Company.

Photo from the collection of CCHS

The morning after the fire, Mr. Weyerhaueser faced the reality of the total loss of the Northern Lumber Company. Gone were their two large sawmills, the planing mill, and sixty to seventy million feet of pine lumber in their storage yards.[101] Despite this great loss, manager Weyerhaeuser knew that he held a significant advantage over the other sawmills. His company had the largest standing timber reserves in northern Minnesota. He was also aware that within a few years the other sawmills would stop operating unless they had a good supply of logs to cut.[102]

Knowing that his forest reserves were crucial to the future of the lumber industry, Weyerhaueser's potential for industry in Cloquet looked promising. With this in mind he set up a meeting with manager Hornby of the Cloquet Lumber Company the day after the fire. A deal was made to have the Cloquet Lumber Company saw the Northern logs and also hire the older employees of the Northern Lumber Company.[103]

The manager of the Cloquet Lumber Company was Henry Hornby.

Photo from the collection of CCHS

The Cloquet Lumber Company was more fortunate as its men were able to save two of its sawmills. As the employees returned to the city, manager Hornby put his crew back to work building camps to house and feed the returning men and whoever was hungry.

As for the Johnson Wentworth Company, it had the least damage of all the sawmills. Although they lost buildings, they were able to immediately call their employees back to work as their plant had not burned. This company became the only source of lumber supply in the city during the time of the rebuilding of the temporary homes since their planer had survived the fire.[105]

How were the men fed once they returned to work?

> The men lived on emergency rations—canned goods, wieners and sardines—heated on the boilers in the engine room. But a camp outfit and camp cook had been summoned by wire (asked to come by telegram) and on Wednesday evening the first warm meals served in the city after the fire were eaten here. The cooking was done in a small shed and the men eating in the open air.[106]

This photo shows several stages in the rebuilding of Cloquet—tents and temporary "fire shacks" can be seen, while more substantial brick buildings are beginning to be built.

Photo from the collection of CCHS

The Northwest Paper Company, a leading manufacturer of newsprint paper, was also untouched. Within a week from the fire the pulp mill was again printing paper. During this time a cook camp was built so free meals could be provided for both employees and non-employees. As many as 1,200 meals were served in a day.[107]

Meanwhile Mr. Hornby and Mr. Weyerhauser hired top wood scientists in the United States to figure out what forest products could be made from "weed trees" (aspen, balsam, and jackpine trees that grew like weeds in the burned down area where the white pine once stood). Finally they developed two new products. One was called balsam-wool, a type of home insulation; and the other was called nu-wood, an artificial lumber used to make ceiling tile and a wall board finish. These products sold well and helped the city survive.[108]

Homes Rebuilt

Incentives for the fire survivors were given to not only return to work in Cloquet, but also to make their home in the city. Gifts of lumber and materials to rebuild temporary homes were provided to sawmill employees who were kept on the company's payroll (money given to employees for their work). Likewise, fire survivors throughout the fire area who were not employees of the sawmill companies received their building materials for temporary homes from the Minnesota Forest Fires Relief Commission. If you were a small family you received material for a 12 ft. by 16 ft. home, while a large family received material for a 12 ft. by 20 ft. home. Some of these buildings still stand today throughout the area and are often times used as garages.

Temporary houses often call "Red Cross Shacks" or "Fire Shacks" were built to house the fire survivors throughout the fire areas.

Photo from the collection of CCHS

Larry Luukkonen recalls what his grandparents had to say of the "fire shacks":

> My grandparents obtained lumber from the sawmills
> with which to build shacks. The uncured lumber was

covered with tar paper to keep the wind out. There was no insulation. The sole means of heat was a wood stove. Lighting was provided by kerosene lamps. Sanitary facilities consisted of a crude privy [outhouse] situated in the backyard. They had no running water. Grandpa Art obtained water from a well in the ruins of great-grandfather Julius' basement. As winter wore on, the uncured lumber began to shrink and cracks appeared in every wall. Blankets were hung in front of windows and doors in an attempt to keep out drafts.[109]

In the year following the fire, new permanent houses were built by the hundreds throughout the fire area. This house is being constructed in Cloquet.

Photo from the collection of CCHS

By the end of December, 1918, most of the fire survivors who had returned to Cloquet were living in homes. A year later there were 1,037 homes of which 534 homes were permanent residences and 503 were temporary buildings.[110] Although the rebirth of the town of Cloquet was incredible, it took many years to recover its population. At the time of the fire its population was estimated to be between 8,000-9,000 people. Two years after the fire the population dropped to 5,127 people. It wasn't until twenty years later that it reached its pre-fire figure. [111]

Cloquet Schools Reopened

Of the five schools in Cloquet only the Garfield School remained standing. At first the school was turned into a flu hospital. Later the hospital was relocated to the Northeastern Hotel on Dunlap Island. Even before the fire leveled the town, all of the schools had been tem-

Garfield School was the only school in Cloquet to survive the fire. It was used as a temporary hospital after the fire and later all of Cloquet's classes were held at Garfield.

Photo from the collection of CCHS

porarily closed due to the Spanish Influenza epidemic. When Garfield School reopened on December 9th, it served 557 children from grade school through high school. It had two shifts. The morning shift was from 8:00 a.m. to 12:00 noon for grade school students while the afternoon shift ran from 12:15 p.m. to 4:15 p.m. for high school students. Teachers lived in the school. They slept in cloak rooms on cots provided by the Red Cross and ate in the school cafeteria.[112]

Trees Replanted

Most of the trees lining the streets of Cloquet were destroyed by the fire. One miraculous exception was Pinehurst Park, where only a few trees were killed. The city took prompt action to reforest the city by obtaining "5,000 fine elms, box elders and soft maples. These were sold at cost to the property owners and were planted on the lots."[113]

Fond du Lac Ojibwe Receive Relief

Upon returning to the Fond du Lac Reservation, the Ojibwe faced the reality of the fire's destruction. Gone was the Indian Village, the Holy Family Church, and many of their farms, homes, livestock, and feed. Left standing were the Indian Hospital and the Indian Farm. Many of the Ojibwe upon returning to the Fond du Lac Reservation stopped first at the Indian Hospital. Here they were fed, given shelter, and treated for burns and injuries. The Indian Farm was used to feed the livestock.[114]

On the day after the fire Superintendent George Cross of the Office of Indian Affairs sent a telegram to the office in Washington, DC for help. The immediate response to his request was $5,000 to buy "flour, groceries, beds, mattresses, blankets, emergency supplies," and rough lumber to build temporary homes. By the summer of 1919 they received $60,000 from the U.S. Congress solely for the building or purchase of homes. The request for money to rebuild barns and outbuildings was refused.[115]

Rebuilding in the Region

Although many lives, farms, and summer homes had been lost in the area around Duluth, the economy of the city was not damaged greatly by the fire. However economic damage was much greater in the farming areas that were burned out. Because harvested crops, seed supplies, livestock, and farm buildings were lost, farmers needed help right away. Aid was given to farmers in the area around Duluth. The *Duluth News Tribune* reported on October 25 that a large, eighty-five foot long community barn had been built at the St. Louis County Work Farm where surviving livestock could be taken care of and "comfortably housed before winter seriously sets in."[116]

By 1923, buildings on the main street of the town of Kettle River had been rebuilt.

Photo from the collection of CCHS

The Red Cross and Relief Commission helped farmers throughout the area build new houses and barns and feed livestock. They also distributed seeds and farm tools. Fire survivor, George Maijala, spoke of the importance of this help, "I cannot praise the efforts of the American Red Cross too highly. They were in the area the next day, with food and clothing and I had my first taste of peanut butter, canned beans and tomatoes. Temporary shelters, tools and building material came later. I was still wearing a Red Cross sweater the following winter..."[117]

After the extensive loss of livestock, an improvement of the dairy herds of the area took place when lost cattle were replaced by purebred Guernseys or Holsteins. H. C. Hanson of Barnum was a leader in the re-establishment of dairy herds and improvement of egg and poultry production in Carlton County. [118]

On May 23, 1919, the *Carlton County Vidette,* in an article headlined, FREE HENS TO FIRE SUFFERERS, wrote that "the relief commission has decided to furnish the settlers who were burned out, with pullets or hens." Because farmers were short of cash after the fire, the cooperative (joining together for a common good) movement grew in the area. Retail co-op stores and dairies flouished in Kettle River, Wright, Moose Lake, Cromwell, and Cloquet. The number of people farming in Carlton County actually grew in the ten years following the fire.[119]

Transportation and utility services were restored quite quickly and Moose Lake had telephone service again by the evening of October 13th. The school building in Moose Lake was one of the few buildings that did not burn and it was used by the military troops and Red Cross right after the fire as a headquarters for relief. After they moved out of the the school, classes began again on January 6, 1919. Rebuilding of homes and businesses in Moose Lake began immediately. Many of the supplies needed in the recovery effort were purchased from local businesses by the Relief Commission. This helped the small businesses to build up again and contributed to the economic regrowth of Moose Lake and other small communities such as Kettle River.[120]

Within a few years of the fire, Moose Lake once again had a busy main street.

Photo from the collection of CCHS

Fire Losses Brought to Court

As the fire refugees returned, the question of "What caused the fires?" and "Who should be held responsible for the damage?" was on everyone's mind. Investigations soon followed. The opinion of most of the public was that the fires were caused by the railroads. As a result, lawsuits were brought against the railroad companies in early 1919. The Northern Minnesota Fire Sufferers Association was also formed in 1919 to help the survivors with their legal claims.

The first few court cases brought against the railroads resulted in failure. All of them involved claims by farmers in outlying areas. However, on September 11, 1920, a major victory in the so-called "Cloquet case" was won. On that day the district court in Duluth declared that the Cloquet fire was caused by the Great Northern Railroad.[121]

Even when the court cases in Minnesota ruled in favor of the fire survivors, the railroad companies refused to pay them. It took as many as seventeen years before payments reached the fire survivors. This was partly due to the large number of claims filed. As many as 15,003 cases were brought against the various railroads in the region during the first few years after the fire.[122]

The other reason for delayed settlement claims for the fire survivors was that the railroad companies decided to take the cases to the Supreme Court in hopes that the court decision would reverse in their favor. On August 29, 1921, the Railroad Administration (an organization created by Congress to direct railroad traffic across the nation during World War I) decided that the 278 fire survivors who had already won their court cases would receive 50% of their total claim. As for the remaining 2,600 Cloquet cases that were yet untried in the courts, they would receive only 40%. The view of the railroad companies was that the fire survivors could "take it or leave it." Although unhappy by the amount of money offered to them, the fire survivors accepted it. Their attitude was "There is nothing we can do. We have no insurance money to rebuild our homes. We have no money to pay for the expensive legal fees of a court case against the powerful Railroad Administration."[123]

Meanwhile Frank Yetka, a Cloquet lawyer, and Anna Dickie Olesen, a Cloquet fire survivor and well known speaker, saw the 50/40% offer by the Railroad Administration as a terrible injustice to the fire survivors. With a strong conviction to represent the fire survivors, they lost no time in testifying before Congress.

In a stirring and passionate speech before Congress, Anna Dickie Olesen had this to say:

Anna Dickie Olesen addressed Congress on behalf of the fire sufferers.

Photo from the collection of CCHS

> I hope we are here to support the right; and not only the right but the courts of Minnesota. We have no right to take a cent of Government money unless the money is rightfully coming to us. Our courts of Minnesota said that my home was burned 100 percent by the agents of the railroad administration. But when I came to get my money back, I get only half, although my house was burned altogether, not half; they burned all my house, not half. They burned everything we had, not half of what we had; and we feel in right and justice and equity we should have that money back.[124]

Even though Olesen's speech failed to get Congress to provide money for the fire survivors, her efforts combined with those of many others, paid off four years later. On August 27, 1935, President Franklin Delano Roosevelt signed the bill for fire survivors to receive the second half of the fire money.[125]

For the fire survivors the Great Fires of 1918 would never be forgotten. Their stories would continue to be told and retold to their families and for many generations to come.

Much rebuilding had gone on in Cloquet by the time this photograph was taken one year after the fire in 1919. Many permanent houses and businesses were built during the first year after the fire.

Photo by Olaf Olson from the collection of CCHS

Five years after the fire, trees and grass are again visible in Cloquet. Schools, churches, the library, and many homes had been built when Olaf Olson took this photograph in 1923.

Photo from the collection of CCHS

The final settlement between the government and the fire sufferers was signed by President Franklin Roosevelt in 1935. The Pine Knot celebrated the settlement with this page in the December 6, 1935, issue.

Photo from the collection of CCHS

GLOSSARY

American Red Cross - an organization in the United States whose purpose is to provide disaster relief to people. This includes clothing, food, shelter, and medical supplies.

Barrracks - a building or group of buildings used for temporary living

Catastrophic Event - a terrible disaster

Crown Fire - fire which explodes into the tops of trees

Cutover Lands - area of land cleared from trees

Divert - to cause something to go in a different course or direction

Erratic - wandering, having no regular or fixed course

Exodus - a large-scale departure of people

Firebrands - flaming pine cones or other debris

Firebreak - a strip of cleared land used to stop the spread of fire

Gondola Car - a shallow, open, railroad car used for freight

Grip - suitcase

Harrowing - extremely distressing, tormenting

Looters - people who steal property or goods especially in times of war or natural disasters such as fires

Humidity - dampness, especially of the air

Motor Corps - A unit of uniformed volunteers of the Minnesota Home Guard which offered their private automobiles as a means of transporting the Home Guard to any point within the state. They also provided transportation for the rescuers, the injured, the National Guardsmen, and volunteer firefighters.

Planing Mill - a machine that smooths the surface of rough lumber

Profiteers - One who makes excessive profits on goods that are in short supply.

Relief - help or assistance especially money, food, shelter, and other necessities, given to the needy or homeless

Refugees - people who are fleeing from danger and seeking a place that provides protection or shelter

Siding - platform where large amounts of pulpwood, cordwood, railroad ties, fence posts, and telephone poles were loaded

Slash - branches and other matter left on a forest floor after the cutting of timber

Trestle - A framework made of vertical, slanted supports, and horizontal crosspieces holding up a bridge

Red Cross nurses and National Guardsmen come to the aid of a fire victim.

Photo by Hugh McKenzie from the collection of CCHS

NOTES TO THE TEXT

INTRODUCTION
1. Carroll, Francis M. and Franklin R. Raiter. *The Fires of Autumn: The Cloquet-Moose Lake Disaster of 1918*. St. Paul: Minnesota Historical Society Press, 1990, p. 4.

CHAPTER ONE
2. Carman, John. "Half a Century Ago Minnesota Burned." *Duluth Sunday News-Tribune*. October 6, 1968, p.2.
3. Carroll, Francis M. *Crossroads in Time: A History of Carlton County, Minnesota*. Cloquet, MN: Carlton County Historical Society, 1987, p. 224.
4. Carroll, Francis M. and Franklin R. Raiter. *The Fires of Autumn: The Cloquet-Moose Lake Disaster of 1918*, p. 8.
5. Interview with Chuck Kramer, Forester, Cloquet Forestry Center. January 27, 2003.
6. Carroll, Francis M. and Franklin R. Raiter. *The Fires of Autumn: The Cloquet-Moose Lake Disaster of 1918*, p. 180.
7. Carroll, Francis M. and Franklin R. Raiter. *The Fires of Autumn: The Cloquet-Moose Lake Disaster of 1918*, p. 77.
8. Carroll, Francis M. and Franklin R. Raiter. *The Fires of Autumn: The Cloquet-Moose Lake Disaster of 1918*, p. 11.
9. Rockvam, Wendy. "Could It Happen Again Today?" *Pine Knot-Billboard*, October 11, 1984, p. 3.

CHAPTER TWO
10. Carroll, Francis M. and Franklin R. Raiter. *The Fires of Autumn: The Cloquet-Moose Lake Disaster of 1918*, p. 26.
11. Carroll, Francis M. and Franklin R. Raiter. *The Fires of Autumn: The Cloquet-Moose Lake Disaster of 1918*, p. 27.
12. Carroll, Francis M. and Franklin R. Raiter. *The Fires of Autumn: The Cloquet-Moose Lake Disaster of 1918*, p. 27.
13. Carroll, Francis M. and Franklin R. Raiter. *The Fires of Autumn: The Cloquet-Moose Lake Disaster of 1918*, p. 27.
14. Carroll, Francis M. and Franklin R. Raiter. *The Fires of Autumn: The Cloquet-Moose Lake Disaster of 1918*, p. 27.
15. Carroll, Francis M. and Franklin R. Raiter. *The Fires of Autumn: The Cloquet-Moose Lake Disaster of 1918*, p. 29.
16. Carroll, Francis M. and Franklin R. Raiter. *The Fires of Autumn: The Cloquet-Moose Lake Disaster of 1918*, p. 29.
17. Johnson, Elizabeth McCamus. CCHS manuscript, unpublished.
18. Clark, Mark. "October 12, 1918. Cloquet, Minnesota. How Were Thousands Saved From the Awfullest Fire Horror in State's History"? April 27, 1999, unpublished manuscript, p. 2.
19. Carroll, Francis M. and Franklin R. Raiter. *The Fires of Autumn: The Cloquet-Moose Lake Disaster of 1918*, p. 32.
20. Alberg, Eva. "1918 Fire Family Story." CCHS manuscript.
21. Peacock, Thomas. *A Forever Story: The People and Community of the Fond du Lac Reservation*. Cloquet, MN: Fond du Lac Band of Lake Superior Chippewa, 1998, p. 75.
22. Carroll, Francis M. and Franklin R. Raiter. *The Fires of Autumn: The Cloquet-Moose Lake Disaster of 1918*, p. 66.
23. Carroll, Francis M. and Franklin R. Raiter. *The Fires of Autumn: The Cloquet-Moose Lake Disaster of 1918*, p. 60.
24. Letter of Sherman Coy. October 17, 1918, CCHS manuscript.

CHAPTER THREE
25. Carroll, Francis M. and Franklin R. Raiter. *The Fires of Autumn: The Cloquet-Moose Lake Disaster of 1918*, p. 43-45.
26. Blinn, Ada Martin. "My Experiences in the Cloquet, Minnesota Fire: October 12, 1918", CCHS manuscript, p. 1.

27. Carroll, Francis M. and Franklin R. Raiter. *The Fires of Autumn: The Cloquet-Moose Lake Disaster of 1918*, p.46.
28. Harney, Rosella. "Rosella Harney Relates Fire Experience". *Pine-Knot Billboard*, October 11, 1984.
29. Lavasseur, Marie. "Sister Remembers the Fire." *Pine-Knot Billboard*, October 11, 1984.
30. Carroll, Francis M. and Franklin R. Raiter. *The Fires of Autumn: The Cloquet-Moose Lake Disaster of 1918*, p. 46.
31. Carroll, Francis M. and Franklin R. Raiter. *The Fires of Autumn: The Cloquet-Moose Lake Disaster of 1918*, p. 46.
32. Lavasseur, Marie. "Sister Remembers the Fire." *Pine-Knot Billboard*, October 11, 1984, p. 3.
33. Harney, Rosella. "Rosella Harney Relates Fire Experience." *Pine-Knot Billboard*, October 11, 1984.
34. Carroll, Francis M. and Franklin R. Raiter. *The Fires of Autumn: The Cloquet-Moose Lake Disaster of 1918*, p. 48.
35. Carroll, Francis M. and Franklin R. Raiter. *The Fires of Autumn: The Cloquet-Moose Lake Disaster of 1918*, p. 48.
36. Lavasseur, Marie. "Sister Remembers the Fire." *Pine-Knot Billboard*, October 11, 1984, p. 3.
37. Carroll, Francis M. and Franklin R. Raiter. *The Fires of Autumn: The Cloquet-Moose Lake Disaster of 1918*, p. 49.
38. Blinn, Ada Martin. "My Experiences in the Cloquet, Minnesota Fire: October 12, 1918", CCHS manuscript, p. 3.
39. Carroll, Francis M. and Franklin R. Raiter. *The Fires of Autumn: The Cloquet-Moose Lake Disaster of 1918*, p. 50.
40. Erickson, Evelyn Elizabeth. "The Cloquet Fire of 1918", CCHS manuscript, p. 3.
41. Erickson, Betty Bergman, "Nineteen-Eighteen," CCHS manuscript, p. 5.
42. Winona, MN: newspaper clipping, CCHS collection.
43. Carroll, Francis M. and Franklin R. Raiter. *The Fires of Autumn: The Cloquet-Moose Lake Disaster of 1918*, p. 52, 55.
44. Carroll, Francis M. and Franklin R. Raiter. *The Fires of Autumn: The Cloquet-Moose Lake Disaster of 1918*, p. 56.
45. Carroll, Francis M. and Franklin R. Raiter. *The Fires of Autumn: The Cloquet-Moose Lake Disaster of 1918*, p. 49.
46. Drew, Mrs. Herbert. "Prize Essay Recalls Fire Horrors On Anniversary." *Pine-Knot Billboard*, October 8, 1937, 2nd Section, p. 1.
47. Blinn, Ada Martin. "My Experiences in the Cloquet, Minnesota Fire: October 12, 1918", CCHS manuscript, p. 3.
48. Carroll, Francis M. and Franklin R. Raiter. *The Fires of Autumn: The Cloquet-Moose Lake Disaster of 1918*, p. 54.
49. Carroll, Francis M. and Franklin R. Raiter. *The Fires of Autumn: The Cloquet-Moose Lake Disaster of 1918*, p. 56.
50. *Pine-Knot*, October, 1919.
51. Carroll, Francis M. and Franklin R. Raiter. *The Fires of Autumn: The Cloquet-Moose Lake Disaster of 1918*, p. 109.
52. "Family's Thrilling Escape From Cloquet Fire Recited." *Duluth Store News*. July 9, 1936.
53. Carroll, Francis M. and Franklin R. Raiter, *The Fires of Autumn: The Cloquet-Moose Lake Disaster of 1918*, p. 111.
54. Blinn, Ada Martin. "My Experiences in the Cloquet, Minnesota Fire: October 12, 1918," p. 4.
55. Lavasseur, Marie. "Sister Remembers the Fire." *Pine-Knot Billboard*, October 11, 1984 p. 10.
56. "One Who Then Was A Wee Girl Recalls Cloquet Fire." *Pine Knot*, December, 1935, p. 1.
57. *Pine-Knot*, October 10, 1919, p.1.
58. Carroll, Francis M. and Franklin R. Raiter. *The Fires of Autumn: The Cloquet-Moose Lake Disaster of 1918*, p. 111.
59. Carroll, Francis M. and Franklin R. Raiter. *The Fires of Autumn: The Cloquet-Moose Lake Disaster of 1918*, p. 118.
60. Drew, Pearl. "The Forest Fire of 1918." CCHS manuscript, p. 5.

61. Lavasseur, Marie. "Sister Remembers the Fire." *Pine-Knot Billboard*, October 11, 1984 p. 10.
62. Carroll, Francis M. and Franklin R. Raiter. *The Fires of Autumn: The Cloquet-Moose Lake Disaster of 1918*, p. 113.
63. Lavasseur, Marie. "Sister Remembers the Fire." *Pine-Knot Billboard*, October 11, 1984 p. 10.
64. Carroll, Francis M. and Franklin R. Raiter. *The Fires of Autumn: The Cloquet-Moose Lake Disaster of 1918*, p. 115.

CHAPTER FOUR
65. Carroll, Francis M. and Franklin R. Raiter. *The Fires of Autumn: The Cloquet-Moose Lake Disaster of 1918*, p. 60, 62.
66. *The Duluth Herald*, October 14, 1918.
67. Carroll, Francis M. and Franklin R. Raiter. *The Fires of Autumn: The Cloquet-Moose Lake Disaster of 1918*, p. 69, 70.
68. *The Duluth Herald*, October 14, 1918, p. 4.
69. Clover Valley/French River History Committee. *Roots in the Past—Seeds for the Future: The Heritage and History of Clover Valley, French River and Surrounding Communities*. Duluth, MN: North Shore Elementary School. 2000, p. 143.
70. Clover Valley/French River History Committee. *Roots in the Past—Seeds for the Future: The Heritage and History of Clover Valley, French River and Surrounding Communities,* p. 148.
71. Carroll, Francis M. and Franklin R. Raiter. *The Fires of Autumn: The Cloquet-Moose Lake Disaster of 1918*, p. 73, 74.

CHAPTER FIVE
72. Carroll, Francis M. and Franklin R. Raiter. *The Fires of Autumn: The Cloquet-Moose Lake Disaster of 1918*, p. 75, 77.
73. Carroll, Francis M. and Franklin R. Raiter. *The Fires of Autumn: The Cloquet-Moose Lake Disaster of 1918*, p. 78.
74. Alanen, Arnold R., ed., *The 1918 Fire in Eastern Aitkin County: Personal Accounts of Survivors*. unpublished manuscript. 1970, p. 6, 7.
75. Alanen, Arnold R., ed., *The 1918 Fire in Eastern Aitkin County: Personal Accounts of Survivors*, p. 8.
76. Alanen, Arnold R., ed., *The 1918 Fire in Eastern Aitkin County: Personal Accounts of Survivors*, p. 8.
77. Hanna, C. A., "Remember the Moose Lake Fire." *Conservation Volunteer*. September-October, 1961, p. 57.
78. Reed, Daniel. *Automba: A Study of a Finnish Timber Boomtown*. Kettle River, MN: Automba Publishing, 1990, p. 61.
79. Manni, Edwin E. *Kettle River, Automba, Kalevala and Surrounding Area History*. self-published. 1978, p. 99.
80. Manni, Edwin E. *Kettle River, Automba, Kalevala and Surrounding Area History*, p. 84.
81. Carroll, Francis M. and Franklin R. Raiter. *The Fires of Autumn: The Cloquet-Moose Lake Disaster of 1918*, p. 90.
82. Buczynski, John A. "Thank You Mother, For Being My Hero," CCHS manscript, p. [4].
83. Erickson, Betty Bergman, "Nineteen-Eighteen," CCHS manuscript, p. [4].
84. *Star Gazette*, October 10, 1968. p. 7, 10.
85. *Superior Telegram*, October 14, 1918.
86. *Star Gazette*, October 10, 1968
87. Manni, Edwin E. *Kettle River, Automba, Kalevala and Surrounding Area History*, p. 119, from *Star Gazette*, October 10, 1968.

CHAPTER SIX
88. Gray, Kathryn Elfes. "50 Years of Progress Since 1918 Holocaust." *Pine Knot*, October 10, 1968.
89. "Cloquet, Home of White Pine." *Pine-Knot Billboard*, October 10, 1919
90. Carroll, Francis M. and Franklin R. Raiter. *The Fires of Autumn: The Cloquet-Moose Lake Disaster of 1918*, p. 105.

91. Carroll, Francis M. and Franklin R. Raiter. *The Fires of Autumn: The Cloquet-Moose Lake Disaster of 1918*, p. 105.
92. Carroll, Francis M. and Franklin R. Raiter. *The Fires of Autumn: The Cloquet-Moose Lake Disaster of 1918*, p. 106.
93. Carroll, Francis M. and Franklin R. Raiter. *The Fires of Autumn: The Cloquet-Moose Lake Disaster of 1918*, p. 108.
94. Carroll, Francis M. and Franklin R. Raiter. *The Fires of Autumn: The Cloquet-Moose Lake Disaster of 1918*, p. 116-117.
95. *Pine Knot*, October 10, 1919, p. 1.
96. Carroll, Francis M. and Franklin R. Raiter. *The Fires of Autumn: The Cloquet-Moose Lake Disaster of 1918*, p. 119.
97. Carroll, Francis M. and Franklin R. Raiter. *The Fires of Autumn: The Cloquet-Moose Lake Disaster of 1918*, p. 121-123.
98. Carroll, Francis M. and Franklin R. Raiter. *The Fires of Autumn: The Cloquet-Moose Lake Disaster of 1918*, p. 56.
99. Carroll, Francis M. and Franklin R. Raiter. *The Fires of Autumn: The Cloquet-Moose Lake Disaster of 1918*, p. 180.
100. Carroll, Francis M. and Franklin R. Raiter. *The Fires of Autumn: The Cloquet-Moose Lake Disaster of 1918*, p. 180.
101. Carroll, Francis M. and Franklin R. Raiter. *The Fires of Autumn: The Cloquet-Moose Lake Disaster of 1918*, p. 181.
102. "Cloquet, Home of White Pine." *Pine-Knot*, October 10, 1919.
103. "Cloquet, Home of White Pine." *Pine-Knot*, October 10, 1919.
104. "Cloquet, Home of White Pine." *Pine-Knot*, October 10, 1919.
105. "Cloquet, Home of White Pine." *Pine-Knot*, October 10, 1919.
106. "Cloquet, Home of White Pine." *Pine-Knot*, October 10, 1919.
107. "Cloquet, Home of White Pine." *Pine-Knot*, October 10, 1919.
108. Carroll, Francis M. and Franklin R. Raiter, *The Fires of Autumn: The Cloquet-Moose Lake Disaster of 1918*, p. 119.
109. Luukkonen, Larry. "Memories of the Fire." CCHS manuscript, p. [3-4].
110. "Cloquet, Home of White Pine." *Pine-Knot*, October 10, 1919.
111. Carroll, Francis M. and Franklin R. Raiter. *The Fires of Autumn: The Cloquet-Moose Lake Disaster of 1918*, p. 187.
112. Olesen, Peter. "Cloquet Schools," *Pine Knot*, October 10, 1919.
113. "Farmers Are Rebuilding Their Homes," *Pine Knot*, October 10, 1919.
114. Carroll, Francis M. and Franklin R. Raiter. *The Fires of Autumn: The Cloquet-Moose Lake Disaster of 1918*, p. 126.
115. Carroll, Francis M. and Franklin R. Raiter. *The Fires of Autumn: The Cloquet-Moose Lake Disaster of 1918*, p. 126-127.
116. *Duluth News Tribune*, October 25, 1918.
117. Manni, Edwin E. *Kettle River, Automba, Kalevala and Surrounding Area History*, p. 83.
118. Carroll, Francis M. and Franklin R. Raiter. *The Fires of Autumn: The Cloquet-Moose Lake Disaster of 1918*, p. 178.
119. Carroll, Francis M. and Franklin R. Raiter. *The Fires of Autumn: The Cloquet-Moose Lake Disaster of 1918*, p. 178, 179.
120. Carroll, Francis M. and Franklin R. Raiter. *The Fires of Autumn: The Cloquet-Moose Lake Disaster of 1918*, p. 179.
121. Carroll, Francis M. and Franklin R. Raiter. *The Fires of Autumn: The Cloquet-Moose Lake Disaster of 1918*, p. 141.
122. Carroll, Francis M. and Franklin R. Raiter. *The Fires of Autumn: The Cloquet-Moose Lake Disaster of 1918*, p. 134.
123. Carroll, Francis M. and Franklin R. Raiter. *The Fires of Autumn: The Cloquet-Moose Lake Disaster of 1918*, p. 148.
124. Fahlstrom, Paul. *Anna Dickie and Peter Olesen: Notable Citizens of Cloquet*: Cloquet, MN: Carlton County Historical Society. 1999, p. 13, 19.
125. Fahlstrom, Paul. *Anna Dickie and Peter Olesen: Notable Citizens of Cloquet* p. 20.
126. Carroll, Francis M. and Franklin R. Raiter. *The Fires of Autumn: The Cloquet-Moose Lake Disaster of 1918*, p. 187.

BIBLIOGRAPHY

Alberg, Eva. "1918 Fire Family Story." ms. Carlton County Historical Society, Cloquet, MN.

Blinn, Ada Martin. "My Experiences in the Cloquet, Minnesota, Fire. October 12, 1918." ms. Carlton County Historical Society, Cloquet, MN.

Buczynski, John A. "Thank You Mother, For Being My Hero." ms. Carlton County Historical Society, Cloquet, MN.

Carman, John. "Half a Century Ago Minnesota Burned." *Duluth Sunday News-Tribune*, October 6, 1968.

Carroll, Francis M. and Franklin R. Raiter. *The Fires of Autumn: The Cloquet-Moose Lake Disaster of 1918*. St. Paul: Minnesota Historical Society Press, 1990.

Carroll, Francis M. *Crossroads in Time: A History of Carlton County, Minnesota*. Cloquet, MN: Carlton County Historical Society, 1987.

Clark, Mark. "October 12, 1918. Cloquet, Minnesota. How Were Thousands Saved From the Awfullest Fire Horror in State's History?" ms. Carlton County Historical Society, Cloquet, MN. April 27, 1999.

Clover Valley/French River History Committee. *Roots in the Past—Seeds for the Future: The Heritage and History of Clover Valley, French River and Surrounding Communities*. Duluth, MN: North Shore Elementary School. 2000.

Drew, Pearl [Mrs. Herbert]. "The Forest Fire of 1918."; Erickson, Evelyn Elizabeth. "The Cloquet Fire of 1918."; Luomala, Katharine. "The Cloquet Fire, October 12, 1918." *A Group of Essays Written by Cloquet Fire Sufferers*. Compiled by The Women's Friday Club. Cloquet, MN: The Women's Friday Club, 1936.

Drew, Mrs. Herbert. "Prize Essay Recalls Fire Horrors on Anniversary." *Pine Knot*. October 8, 1937, Second Section.

Duluth News Tribune and *Duluth Herald* newspapers of October, 1918.

Fahlstrom, Paul. *Anna Dickie and Peter Olesen: Notable Citizens of Cloquet*. Cloquet, MN: Carlton County Historical Society, 1996.

"Family's Thrilling Escape From Cloquet Fire Recited." *Duluth Store News*. July 9, 1936: n.pg.

Forest Fire Planning Committee. *The Great 1918 Forest Fire Museum and Heritage Center: Planning Study*. Cloquet, MN: Forest Fire Planning Committee, 1993.

"Forest Fire Sweeps Cloquet." *Potlatch Story*. San Francisco: Potlatch Corporation, April 23, 1969.

The Fury of the Flames: A Pictorial Record of the Great Forest Fires Which Raged in Northern Minnesota, Oct. 12-15, 1918. Duluth: Martin A. Olmem, 1919.

Gray, Kathryn Elfes. "50 Years of Progress Since 1918 Holocaust." *Pine-Knot*. October 10, 1968.

Hanna, C.A. "Remember the Moose Lake Fire." *Conservation Volunteer*, September-October, 1961.

Harney, Rosella. "Rosella Harney Relates Fire Experience." *Pine Knot-Billboard*. October 11, 1984.

Johnson, Elizabeth McCamus. ms. Carlton County Historical Society; Cloquet, MN. n.d.

Lavasseur, Marie. "Sister Remembers the Fire." *Pine Knot-Billboard*. October 11, 1984.

Lumppio, Saima. "Saima's Story." ms. Carlton County Historical Society; Cloquet, MN. n.d.

Luukkonen, Arnold L. "Brave Men in Their Motor Machines--And the 1918 Forest Fire." *Ramsey County History*. Fall, 1972.

Luukkonen, Larry. "Memories of the Fire." ms. Carlton County Historical Society; Cloquet, MN. n.d.

Manni, Edwin E. *Kettle River, Automba, Kalevala and Surrounding Area History*. self-published, 1978.

Minnesota Forest Fires Relief Commission. *Final Report*. Duluth, MN: 1921.

"One Who Then Was A Wee Girl Recalls Cloquet Fire." *Pine-Knot*. December, 1935.

Peacock, Thomas. *A Forever Story: The People and Community of the Fond du Lac Reservation*. Cloquet, MN: Fond du Lac Band of Lake Superior Chippewa, 1998.

Piippo-Lambert, Carol Illikainen. *Firebeast: The Fires of 1918*. Moose Lake, MN: Moose Lake Area Historical Society, 1994.

Pine-Knot. October 10, 1919.

Reed, Daniel. *Automba: A Study of a Finnish Boomtown*. Kettle River, MN: Automba Publishing, 1990.

Rockvam, Wendy. "Could the Disaster Happen Again?" *Pine Knot-Billboard*. October 11, 1984.

Rogers, Harold. "Minnesota's Flaming Terror." *Coronet*, November, 1948.

"Villages Burn, People Perish." *The Hinckley Enterprise*, October 18, 1918.

FIRE STORIES

There were many stories told about the fires—sad, exciting, scary, and even funny. Everyone who lived through the fire had a story to tell about their own experiences during the fire and after the fire. Many people wrote down their stories to share with their families and others. Stories were handed down in families—told and retold to the children. Many of these stories were written down later by others. This is a short collection of some interesting fire stories. Other stories have been collected into books. A list of suggested readings on page 121 gives information about these books.

One Who Then Was A Wee Girl Recalls Cloquet Fire

An anonymous account taken from the *Pine Knot*, Fire Reimbursement Jubilee Edition, December, 1935.

Though I blew out eight candles on my cake the January following, in our little temporary shack-home, every minute of that night of red horror is etched forever on my mind.

I can recall plainly the eerie, brassy sky that afternoon when the sun hung like a red Christmas-tree ball in the sky. I can remember the unspoken apprehension of my mother as she busied herself with the usual Saturday baking and scrubbing; can see again grandmother as she knelt in her bedroom, her aged lips moving softly in prayer. And—how plainly I recall that unforgettable "forest-fire" odor.

How plainly I remember that last supper in that kitchen with its shining black wood range, the brown and yellow linoleum of the floor, the square table whereon all meals, except those of special occasion, were eaten. I can still bring back plainly the picture of mother, in an ankle-length "bungalow apron" of blue and white checked gingham, taking the freshly baked bread out of the oven and bemoaning the war with its flour substitutes that had prevented the loaves from raising properly. In spite of the red glow spreading across the western sky as evening came on, we ate our supper—we had beef stew with vegetables and dumplings—while brother pounded on his high chair with his spoon. While mother "did up" the supper work, grandma prepared brother for bed and set me to undressing myself for a Saturday night bath in a round washtub in front of the kitchen range, and father went out to talk over this "fire scare" with the neighbors. Grandma bade me watch brother lest he roll off the bed while she went to the kitchen to warm his bottle. While we were alone, the lights went out! I screamed with the terror of childhood, but soon grandma, coming with a candle, reassured me.

Just as I was stripped to my underwear and mother was filling the tub with warm water from the reservoir of the stove, father burst in—his usually placid features distorted with fear. "Get that kid dressed, Lucille, and you, mother, get the baby wrapped up and get your own coats on. We're getting out of here." "Getting out—what do you mean?" asked mother incredulously. "I mean that it looks like this whole town is going up like so much paper and there's a train down at the depot and we're getting in it with these kids."

That wild half hour of packing, remembering the baby's bottles and other necessities, trying to think what would go in the two suitcases (mother never did live down remembering her "western" curlers and forgetting her new fall hat). I begged to wear my new woolen hat embroidered with pink yarn roses ("Don't let her wear that, ma, she'll get it dirty. Put her dark blue on her.") Tucking the sleeping babe in his buggy I tied a Red Riding Hood cape on the cherished doll that Santa Claus had brought only last Christmas. Mother hurrying back to the kitchen to turn the stove damper down (as if it made any difference an hour later), grandma taking a mute farewell of her husband's picture—it was the only one she had of him and it was life-sized and encased in a heavy gilt frame. Mother's query, "Did you hook the back door, Eric?" as she turned the key in the front door. "Yes, I hooked the door, but wait—this kid can't take that doll, she's got to have her hands free to hold onto mother." Back into the house to lay my doll on the sofa—and was assured she'll be there in the morning—and out again into that hurricane of a wind filled with smoke, flying leaves and cinders.

Father carried the two suitcases, mother struggled desperately with the perambulator (baby buggy), and I clung to grandma who carried a bundle of keepsakes in her other hand. Down the street we marched, our neighbors joining us—a steady, silent exodus, marching in time to sirens at the mill shrieking up and down the scale, and that demon of a wind trying to out howl it.

At the depot there was an ore train waiting with an engine intermittently tooting and whistling. "Surely, we can't go in that!" protested mother. "We're lucky to get out of here in anything," answered father as he stopped to lift the baby, with his blankets, into mother's arms.

The fire was plainly to be seen now. Buildings not so far away were in flames—one could hear the roar and hiss of the fire, the howl of the wind, the eerie wail of the siren, the insisting tooting of the locomotive, and the screaming of horses. Long years after, I asked my father why all those horses were there. He answered, "Those were horses that had brought farmers and their families to the train and when the families were once safely aboard there was nothing for the farmers to do but to unharness the poor beasts and leave them to their fate."

As we approached the ore train with its human cargo, we were told to go to the boxcars on the next train. When we reached the boxcar a man picked me up and hoisted me into it. Frantically, I called grandma and as she answered, "I'm coming," she landed beside me on all fours. "Here, Ma, take the baby," called mother, and brother, mercifully still sleeping, was tossed into grandma's arms. Then up came mother, her hat askew, and breathless. Father tossed in the suitcases with the instruction that grandma and mother sit on them. Then, father himself was with us, trying to relieve mother of the burden of holding brother. "No, no," she answered in a tone just bordering on hysteria, "I've gotta keep my hands on him and hold him close to me—you hold sister." Huddled closely together we waited.

Finally the train began to move—slowly. There were no outbursts from the people gathered in that boxcar—an occasional smothered sob, a whispered prayer, but, in general, silence. It seemed we rode hours—then we were at Carlton. Father got out of the train then and stood talking with other men. Finally he came back and climbed in saying, "They say the whole thing's going up good over there," with a nod in the direction of Cloquet.

Mother said nothing but just held the precious burden in her arms a little closer and grandma fished around in her bundle and extracted her knitting. "Have you brought your knitting, of all things?" asked mother. With a lifelong habit of handling the needles, grandma continued to knit answering, "I can get Walter's sox done for his birthday next month."

The next thing I knew I was being lifted off the train and I was cold and sleepy in the midst of strange people—confusion. A man said, "Here is a family with a baby, you take them." A deep kindly voice said, "Let me carry the little girl and you come with me." I remember being carried blocks then into a strange house, and lain on a bed while a woman with tears in her eyes undressed me. The same kindly voice of a man boomed out, "Now you folks lay the little fellow in here while I put the coffee on!"

Then morning to find grandma in bed with me in this unfamiliar room. I stepped out of the bed only to trip on the adult-size nightgown. "Mama, I want to go home to our house and I want Sally-Dolly." "Oh, my darling," sobbed mother, "we have no house, your daddy has no job in the mill—we are homeless."

Ruins of Cloquet are pictured in this Olaf Olson photograph from the collection of CCHS.

Fire Sufferers Remember

A story by Ada Martin Blinn taken from a CCHS Manuscript.

    Could I ever forget it! The awful wind, the smoke and the red flames that swept up over the hill. But let me go back and tell of my supper that stood waiting for my son to come from the office, but who did not come. And although his wife, Ruby, phoned him several times she got no answer. How she spent her time running from door to door, looking first one way and then the other, not saying much, and as I was busy in the kitchen I did not realize how bad it was getting to be. But laughingly said to her, "Well I am hungry, I think I will eat. Then if the town does burn up, I will go out on a full stomach and you will go out hungry."

    At last the phone rang and when Ruby answered it, she turned to me and said, "Ned says pack a few things and prepare to leave at once, people are going as fast as they can and the fire is very near." She then told me to pack a grip (suitcase) with things I thought I would need most for a few days. I was like a child and did just as she told me. Her mind seemed so clear and alert. And when she called to me to do a bundle of bedding, a warm quilt or two and your winter coat, I did it without question. Smiling I remember, and saying to myself as I pulled my bed apart, "I bet I'll be spreading these things back in a few hours..."

    Then Ned BURST thru the door, excitement in every move he made. "Hurry, hurry," he said. "And, Oh, Ruby, how are we going to take the baby out in this wind?" (Lester was about three months old at this time and weighed only...a few...lbs at birth.) "Don't worry," she said, "I can do it." ...And saying always, "Hurry, hurry." I could still hear him out in the street calling, "Come on Ma, what are you doing? You will get separated from us in the crowd." And I answered, "I am trying to find the right switch to turn off the lights in the front room." I also locked the door. When I reached the street, I was surprised at the crowd, every one carrying something. No one seemed to say a word. When I reached the Depot, Ned had just succeeded in getting Ruby and the Baby in a crowded coach. "Come on," he said, "no room for you and me in here." We struggled along the Depot platform and still on to the last car, a gondola they called it. I don't believe it had ever been used it was so clean. . . I seemed to be the first one in the car but it was filling fast. Men, women, and children climbing up the little steps and jumping down inside. As I stood looking over the top of the car, it came just below my chin and I could see people from all sides running to reach the Depot. Some of them were my best friends. This was our only hope of escape. As the train pulled out, I could see a big coal shed just below the Depot burst into flames.

As we started I felt that I was much more comfortable than lots of the others as I sat on the bundle I had put up, while others sat on the bottom of the car. Many of the women were crying and sobbing but on the whole the children were quiet. I have often wondered whether this was the excitement or was it fear? One woman near me kept crying and saying, "Oh, my eyes, my eyes." So I said to her, "Suppose you try not to cry and hold your handkerchief close over them as I am doing, and I think you will find they will feel better." I shall never forget her voice as she cried out, "But I haven't got a handkerchief." I remember that I slipped a pile of handkerchiefs in my grip, I pulled one out and gave it to her; she did as I said. It was well worth the trouble for the crying soon ceased.

We that are used to this country and know how cold it gets in the middle of the night in Oct. will not wonder that when I looked at Ned he was shivering with the cold. He was standing in the middle of the car with children of all sizes sitting so close to him he could not move a foot. I said, "Oh, Ned you are so cold." "Yes, I wish I had taken my overcoat." I gave him my light coat which I was wearing and I got my winter coat from my bundle. We were moving (by train) about as fast as a man could walk, every culvert and bridge we passed over was either on fire or had been. So we were in great danger of a wreck. It was nearly two o'clock in the morning when we reached the Depot in Superior, Wisconsin...I stood up and looked around. Such a sight. People were gathered around that little Depot by the hundreds. And everyone seemed to be so quiet. Occasionally, I could hear someone calling to a friend, and sometimes I heard a sob. People were climbing out of the car as fast as they could...

When I think of people being kind I always think of the people of Superior that night. They did everything they possibly could to get the people under cover and out of the cold. Taking them to their homes, to the churches, to the theaters, and to the schools. A man soon had us all in his car and drove to one of the school buildings. There seemed to be some trouble getting the door unlocked and just then Lester began to cry. "Oh, Ned," Ruby said, "What will we do? It is baby's feeding time." He answered, "I know what I am going to do. I am going across the street where the light is and see if they will take us in." He was soon back saying they were just waiting up to see if they could help some of the fire refugees. As soon as we could get there, hot coffee and lunch was ready and beds were spread for us to sleep in and how we did sleep! We were so tired...

In the early morning, Ned was up and away looking for a chance to get back to Cloquet. As I stood looking out the window, I could see Cloquet people going up and down the school house steps across the way. I told Ruby I would go over and see if I could hear any word from home. As I went up the steps, I met one of the prominent Clergymen of Cloquet. He smiled sadly and held out his hand, saying, "Well Mrs. Blinn, we are here." "But what of home? What of Cloquet?," I said. "Burned to the ground, nothing left." It didn't take me long to get back to Ruby. Gone. Gone. We have no home. And for the first time, I began to cry. And she, brave soul that she was, threw her arms around me and said, "What do we care? We have Ned and the Baby left."

The people of Cloquet returned to scenes of rubble and ash.

Photo from the collection of CCHS

Prize Essay Recalls Fire Horrors on Anniversary
Graphic Story of 1918 Blaze Told In Article

by Mrs. Herb (Pearl) Drew

This essay was one of the winners in the Cloquet Friday Club's essay contest in 1936. It was reprinted in the *Pine Knot* on October 8, 1937.

    A half-holiday! How many things we'd like to do when a surprise such as this comes to us—especially in the fall, when the woods are so gorgeous, the air so balmy, and the trails so inviting. But no! Winter will soon be here, and that means warm clothes must be hunted up, aired, cleaned or mended. Which reminds me of that fox muff I had saved months for—finally it was mine. On that momentous day, it was brought out, admired and anticipated—but never worn. After getting everything on the clothesline, the wind grew to such a gale, that we had to take it all down again, or it would have been whipped to shreds. An unusual wind, carrying dirt, sawdust, leaves and sticks!

    By 3 o'clock, it was as dusky as a summer evening, but there the resemblance ends. There was a queer glow in the sky. What did it mean?

    "Oh," said the old-timers, "Its just a forest fire up the line."

    "But," we remonstrated, "this looks mighty close to us."

    "Nonsense," they laughed, "we've seen lots worse skies than this."

    But the eerie glow grew brighter, and the wind grew stronger—the old-timers' nonchalance seemed foolish. "Perhaps a forest ranger might be able to relieve our fears," we thought. But instead, he said seriously, "There is not danger as long as the wind comes from that direction. But—be ready to leave town on a moment's notice. You never can tell where a forest fire will go."

    Following his advice, I went home and wrote a cheerful, "don't worry" letter to my husband, who was fighting in the Argonne (in World War I) just about that time and had enough worries and fears—then gathered a few choice possessions into a small bag. Did we take the things that cost the most? Indeed not! Values change at a time like this...a class ring, a few pictures, an old locket and chain, the watch he gave me when he sailed for France—little keepsakes that cost so little and mean so much!

"What would a person wear if we did have to leave town? Should I wear my new suit, or put on an old woolen dress? Maybe I'd better take an old coat along too," such were the thoughts that ran through my mind. The warm dress won—also the winter coat and hat.

Supper time, with the sky still ruddier, and the wind howling. Everybody was pacing the floor and asking each other what to do next. A rumor came that Brookston was burning, and that a train full of refugees was already headed for Cloquet. Now the pioneers were beginning to realize the danger, and were gathering their valuable papers and receipts, some burying their silver in trenches in the gardens—hunting keys that would never be used—locking doors that soon were burning!

Seven-thirty! The sky was crimson by this time and firebrands were blowing through the air. Store signs were swinging madly, windows rattled wildly—everything was topsy-turvy!

One has to be moving at a time like this. I begged anyone, everyone to please come with me, away from that awful sky! But where should we go? We would lose our way on a country road—the safest thing to do would be to follow the railroad tracks to Carlton. Finally my friend Effie said she couldn't stay inside any longer, anything would be better than sitting still.

It was only a few blocks to the depot, but the wind was like a cyclone. We dodged flying embers, dirt, loose papers, branches of trees, expecting something to crash down on us any minute. When we reached the depot, we were amazed to find a train waiting to take refugees from our town. It was already packed with women and children. Ah! Our beloved station agent had realized the danger, and held a train so we could get out. We all owe undying gratitude to him, for his thoughtfulness, far-sightedness, and brotherly love. He pushed us up the steps, and told us to get in and stay in, and when we begged to go back and tell the others how serious the situation was, he said, "Don't you worry. Every person in this town will be notified." Boys were sent up and down the streets to warn those still in their homes to get out. We threw our bags on the platform. How could we find our own in that heap? Really, we never expected to see them again.

We pushed our way into the train, already filled with anxious women and children—mothers wondering where their children were, and children crying for their parents—nobody knowing where they were being taken out of danger.

Each person that came in told how much closer the fire was—"The 'Y' was burning"—"Now the houses on Sixth Street were on fire." "The flaming boards were being blown for blocks"—"New fires were starting all over town." Couldn't they start the train? Did we have to be cremated after all? Why can't we go? The coaches were packed, surely there wasn't room for another person. Oh, how trapped we felt!

After an eternity of waiting, we moved. Thank God!

But we just crept along, stopping every couple blocks to pick up more panic-stricken stragglers, who had more hair-raising stories to harass us—"Carlton was burning"—"Fires all along the way"—"Cars in tangled heaps"—"Drivers blinded by smoke and dirt"—How could we hope to get away from it all?

Still the train crawled along. We passed through Carlton, came to the high trestle in Jay Cooke Park, and stopped right in the middle of it. Of all places where we had stopped, this seemed the worst. Fire was everywhere—flames licking from the deep gullies to the very tracks we were on. This was the end—we were sure of it. The rails were so hot, they dared not attempt to put the weight of the engine on them, until they were cooled. Someone came with the news that a sprinkler was being used to cool them. If prayers would help, this was a time when it could be proven, because everyone in that train must have been praying like they never did before. There wasn't a sound! Our prayers were answered. We were moving!

After hours of this stealthy creeping—through many raging grass fires—we came to a full stop. Now what? Where were we? Why, this was a real station, full of lights and people—friendly people, waiting to take us to their home. Families were finding each other—others hunting desperately for ones they hoped had been in a different coach—joy and sorrow intermingled.

I was taken to a nice clean home that would have been perfect at any other time, but they too, were frantic with worry. The fire was out of control in South Superior, so they were getting ready to flee, just as we had. No use trying to rest—might as well get out and try to help the workers in the relief places.

I went to the "Y" where volunteers were making thousands of sandwiches and gallons of coffee. There was plenty to do here. Mattresses were spread over the large "gym" floor, each one haven of a foreign family. They would not be separated for a minute. With their few belongings in a sack, the mother clutched it firmly and would not budge. The family moved as a whole, or not at all. Such a problem!

The next day they gave me the job of checking through lists of refugees, and attempting to get families in touch with each other. Everyone registered somewhere, giving the address of the people who were caring for them. It was hard to recognize some of our best friends —with faces black from smoke and soot, clothes disheveled from their ride in open freight or coal cars. It took days to get the cinders and dirt out of our bloodshot eyes, but—we were alive!

The churches, theaters, schools, and lodges opened their doors wide. Women cooked and donated food—washed countless dishes, made over clothes for children—took care of the sick (and there were so many sick with the flu at this time), everyone giving themselves at this crucial time. Such sympathy, kindness, and unselfishness can never be forgotten.

What was left of Cloquet? Could we go back and see if anything was saved? Not for a few days, at least. Crews were cleaning up the wire-strewn streets, putting guard rails around dangerous smoldering fires, and building barracks for the soldiers who stayed all winter to prevent looting and destruction of property.

On Tuesday, we were permitted to come—and our worst fears were realized. Nothing but desolation! That couldn't be Cloquet! Where were the beautiful trees? Surely the brick buildings couldn't burn to the ground! Even the ashes seemed to have blown away. There wasn't a landmark anywhere that we could recognize—we needed a guide to find our own homes.

Slowly we grasped the meaning of a real forest fire—it leaves nothing but ruin! Chunks of glass—heaps of broken plates and crockery! Wild wires dangling grotesquely—Why, that had been my piano! Masses of tumbled brick, yes, that was all that was left of the new high school.

People walked the barren streets, with tears streaming down their cheeks, discouraged and heart-sick. Why work so hard to get ahead in this world when all you had striven for could be snatched away from you in one fell swoop?

Discouraged? Not for long! This was home—no one wanted to go away. If the mills would open again, they would stay. A shack would do for awhile—and families of six or eight managed to live in a one-room house for months, some for years. Like mushrooms springing up overnight, one shack after another dotted the snow covered city. With smoke curling from the chimneys they looked quaint and inviting snuggled in the snow. Primitive? Yes, but comfortable and friendly.

A home again! One's own fireside—the family together again—everyone so busy that time disappeared like magic. Once more we learned, "Be it ever so humble, there's no place like home."

DON'T LOSE COURAGE!

To Our Friends and Neighbors:

Suffering through a common calamity in which the all-devouring flames spared none, we stand as yet appalled by the tragedy that has destroyed our city and devastated our homes. After the first prayer of thankfulness that Cloquet has been spared the awful loss of human life, such as has been sustained in other localities, to many of us has come the black despair that must come to every people when they face the future homeless and penniless, yet we would say to our Cloquet neighbors to put that despair behind them and let us take up the work of life anew.

Cloquet will arise from its ashes and ruins a better and more beautiful city than it has been in the past. This is the history of Virginia, of Chisholm, and many other towns that have been fire swept in the past.

A message to the people of Cloquet in the Carlton County Vidette *on October 18, 1918.*

History of Cloquet

Excerpts from "History of Cloquet" by Joseph N. Franklin, an unpublished CCHS Manuscript. Mr. Franklin was a mail carrier in Cloquet at the time of the fire.

October 12, 1918...that day was declared a holiday and the whole community was warned as to the danger of forest fires coming in from the Northwest. The day shift at all mills and planers labored all day and some of the night shift were working. At about 8:00 p.m. the fire broke over the hill from the direction of the present golf course into what was known as Squaw or Bottle Alley. In this ravine, all of the lumber from the Northern Mills known as #5 was piled.

Realizing that the town was now doomed, orders to evacuate were then issued. Preparations had been made at the depot. The engines had been held at Cloquet and practically all of the available cars moved in the vicinity of the depot. I was not working on that day and lived on land across from the Caza Home in a small house owned by Alfred Grunig. At about 6:00 p.m., Bob Monroe and his wife stopped on the road and said that things looked bad. There were fires along the road from Duluth to Carlton and the sky in the West was just a red glow. Shortly afterward the cars began to stream by from Cloquet. I took the old car into town and got down to 14th Street and Cloquet Avenue and saw people with all their valuables thrown into sheets heading to the depot. I then turned and drove home and my wife and I loaded the family and necessary clothing in the car and drove to Carlton. We spent the night in the Carlton City Hall. About 4:00 a.m., Archie Campbell, City Engineer, stated that he was driving to Cloquet. We drove to the corner of 14th Street and Carlton Avenue and the entire street, on both sides, was in flames. We turned on the corner of 14th Street and headed back to Carlton.

The following morning we drove to Cloquet arriving at about 8:30 a.m. The entire town was burned, with the exception of the Garfield School which was still standing along with the Gulbranson house to the southeast. The Art Ogren house was standing, which was in the 200 block on 17th Street. There were about 4 houses on the East End on Avenue C which had not burned. The two Northern Mills were burned, but the other mills remained. The wind must have shifted so that the Match Factory was left standing.

The call then went out to return to Cloquet. Company boarding camps were built on the plot now occupied by the Post Office...one on 2nd Street just off the avenue. The Northwest Paper Co. also had a boarding camp, and several houses were built to house their employees.

After the mills began to operate, the lumber companies gave each family $150.00 worth of lumber and shacks were built on their respective lots to house their families.

We opened the Post Office in the Northeastern Hotel in the first part of November and, after we got organized, we found we had too much inside help. The postmaster at that time was Edward S. Scheibe. I [was sent] to Virginia and carried mail for two months—November and December. On New Year's Day I was asked to return to Cloquet as they would start the delivery of mail after New Year's. City delivery was started...and I took over on my old Route #3, Cloquet Avenue and 14th Street East.

In Cloquet rebuilding began among the ruins. Barracks for the returning mill workers, temporary houses, and businesses were quickly built before winter set in.

Photo from the collection of CCHS

Saima's Story

by Saima Lumppio taken from an unpublished CCHS manuscript.
This story was written by Saima many years after the fire, but she remembered her story very clearly.

I was 8 years old, but I can remember just about everything that happened that day...

The wind was blowing hard and things were flying around. The sky was dark, and we could see a glow of light far away from our home. We didn't know what it was, and later on when the wind turned north, we knew it must be something serious.

My mother and older brother, Hans, were milking cows. They let the cows out of the barn because they knew something serious was happening. At that point our Dad was fighting fires at the neighbors. When he noticed that the wind turned north, he hurried home. He just made it in on time to help us...just before the porch collapsed because our house was on fire. There was no way to get out of the house except through a window. Dad knocked the window out and pulled all of us out. It was a terrible feeling to face the sparks, burning wood, and trees.

We all ran to the road. Dad told us to go in the ditch for fresh air. It was smoky and getting dark. We ducked into a ditch every few feet. The last time we went into the ditch two huge bundles of burning hay from our neighbor's hay shed flew on top of my younger sister and me. We struggled unsuccessfully to get out from under that burning hay. The rest of the family didn't know what had happened to us, and they continued running toward a bridge. This bridge spanned a small creek that ran under North Road. Suddenly, Dad noticed that two of his children were missing! He quickly ran back. He discovered my younger sister, Lila, pulling me to safety since I had already lost consciousness. My Dad picked us up and carried each of us under an arm to the safety underneath the bridge.

There were several people under the bridge. The older people thought it would be better to go to the school house across the road for shelter—but then that started burning, too. Then they decided to go to the neighbor's potato field. The buildings there had already burned so it seemed safe from fiery disaster. We all went to the potato fields. I remember my younger sister and I were really in terrible pain. We were burned very badly. The fiery hay had burned our legs, hair, arms, faces, and my side.

My entire family minus brother Hans (who stayed at the cheese factory) went to Duluth to the armory. We stayed there for about 3 days. Dad said I was unconscious then. Finally my sister Lila and I were moved to St. Luke's Hospital into a small room. They clipped our clothes off with scissors because they were so badly burned on our skin. After that we moved into a children's ward. Someone cut our hair because it was almost burned off.

The next day the hospital started our treatments. They were horrible. Every morning they tried to clean our bloody scars which were dirty with dirt from the potato field. They didn't have any medication to stop the pain or the bleeding. One day they put cotton batton on the open sores, and the next morning they would take it off and put warm paraffin wax on. I was in terrible pain. I recall crying for many months each morning after the treatments. Lila and I stayed at St. Luke's Hospital for 5 months.

The fire affected more than just our bodies. During that prolonged stay in the hospital both my Mother and brother George died from influenza. My sister and I also missed the rest of that school year! It was very difficult to catch up when we went back to school in the fall.

When my sister and I were finally released from the hospital in the Spring of 1919, we found out that we didn't have a home. We went to my Auntie's house—Father's sister. We didn't get to go home until Dad built a little house. It was very sad to go home...no Mother, no toys, nothing was the same. Father had to be both a mother and a father! There was nothing much there, but I guess we were glad to be home.

Memories of the Fire

Excerpts from "Memories of the Fire" by Larry Luukkonen taken from a CCHS manuscript which tells about his grandparents' experiences in the fire.

Saturday, October 12th, 1918, began like any other fall day for my maternal grandparents, Amy and Arthur Dobrowolski. They had purchased a new bungalow near the corner of 6th Street and Carlton Avenue. "Grandma Amy" and "Grandpa Art," as they liked to be called, were busy with the myriad tasks confronting new homeowners preparing for winter. Horse-drawn wagons from the sawmill had dumped loads of fresh slabwood in their front yard and my grandparents had "worked like two beavers" bringing it all in and piling it up to the basement ceiling. All that wood and a bin full of coal made them feel very comfortable.

With their winter fuel supply secure, my grandparents turned to other chores such as canning. Everyone canned in those days. With the country at war, "Victory Gardens" could be found in many backyards.

My paternal grandparents, Olga and Emil Luukkonen, were also hard at work. Grandmother Olga was busy Saturday afternoon washing some items while my grandfather was at work. Mindful that her wedding ring might be damaged, she removed it and placed it on the kitchen windowsill. She was very absorbed with her work and forgot about the ring.

No one ever told me exactly how my grandparents received word of the approaching fire. My grandmother Amy noticed how red the sun was. There was a slight smell of smoke in the air, but everyone was used to smelling smoke in the fall. It was the wind that bothered her. She finally decided to go across the street to the neighbors and see what was happening. While crossing the street, a sudden gust of wind completely knocked her off her feet. Soon afterward my grandfather brought word of the fire and the family left for Carlton with the neighbors. Grandma Amy told me many times how she left with my 8 month old mother, Vivian Dobrowolski, and little more than the clothes on their backs. Mother was the first grandchild in the family and had lots of nice baby clothes but, in haste to leave, only a few items were taken.

My mother and grandparents rode in the neighbor's car to Carlton along Highway 4 (14th Street or the "Carlton Road") which was the main thoroughfare into Cloquet from the south. Highway 4 was filled with cars and wagons, so the neighbor had to drive slowly to avoid a collision. They headed south to Highway 2 (the "Moorhead Road") and then on to Carlton.

After arriving at Carlton, my grandfather had to fight fire. My grandmother and mother spent the night in Johnson's Pool Hall where my mother slept on the pool table. In the morning they left by train to join relatives in Superior, Wisconsin.

Meanwhile, my grandfather Emil Luukkonen also heard about the fire danger and rushed home to warn his family. Grandma Olga dropped her washing and packed some things together. My grandparents, my 15 month old father Arnold, and my great-grandparents, Mary and Jacob Luukkonen, all left in Emil's Dodge touring car. Their destination was Olga's parents' farm some two miles east of Cloquet. They arrived safely at the Hugo Sjoblad farm where preparations were underway to save the buildings. Carpets and rugs were placed on the roofs of the buildings and wet down with buckets of water. The fields had been plowed or mowed so everyone felt reasonably safe from the approaching fire.

There are accounts of people who went back to Cloquet to save personal effects (belongings). My great-grandfather, Jacob Luukkonen, heard that his house had not burned; and, remembering he had left his watch at home, he set out on foot for Cloquet. As he turned the corner of Avenue F and 18th Street he could see his house. As he started west along Avenue F, the house suddenly burst into flames! It seemed to explode! Startled by it all he turned and retraced his steps, leaving the fire to consume everything in its path.

After the fire people returned to survey the scene of desolation. My grandparents came back to try to salvage whatever was left. At first it was hard to tell exactly where their houses had been! All they found were smoldering cellar holes. The piles of slabwood and coal, so carefully stored for winter, took several days to burn out. All that was left were a few trinkets, some copper pennies from a bank hopelessly fused together, broken dishes, and twisted metal.

Spirits were raised amid the ruins when it was discovered that my grandfather, Arthur Dobrowolski, had taken his time-books with him. The books were the only records available showing who worked at the sawmill. People were glad to know they would at least be paid for their work and have some money to start over.

Miraculously, my grandmother Olga's wedding ring was found in the ruins of her home. Emil Buskala, the local jeweler, cleaned and repaired the ring. It was the only thing of value recovered from the fire.

In the rush to leave, people left valuables behind. One woman buried her possessions in the garden. After the fire she retrieved everything including an heirloom spinning wheel. I remember watching her spin with it—forty years later! Great-grandfather Julius Dobrowolski feared he had lost his dog to the flames, but much to his relief, his dog returned while Julius was searching the ruins of his home.

My grandparents set about building temporary shelters soon after the fire. They obtained lumber from the sawmills with which to build shacks. The uncured lumber was covered with tar paper to keep the wind out. There was no insulation. The sole means of heat was a wood stove. Lighting was provided by kerosene lamps. Sanitary facilities consisted of a crude privy situated in the backyard. They had no running water. Grandpa Art obtained water from a well in the ruins of great-grandfather Julius' basement.

The Red Cross responded immediately to the disaster with clothes, food, and some basic furnishings which helped make the shacks livable. As winter wore on the uncured lumber began to shrink and cracks appeared in every wall. Blankets were hung in front of windows and doors in an attempt to keep out drafts.

My grandparents didn't take much comfort from the promise of "fire money" to indemnify (to make payment for) their losses. It took years before a claim for a hundred dollars was paid off and then the government discounted the final amount.

All my grandparents survived the fire of 1918 and went on to rebuild their homes and lives.

Night of Flame

Excerpts from a CCHS manuscript by Tina Hakkarainen Pearson.
The Hakkarainen farm was located about five miles north of Esko in Thomson Township. Tina's parents were Charles and Hilda Hakkarainen.

The air smelled of smoke and the sun was a red ball in the sky for weeks. The grownups talked of fire to the north and northwest. The old mother cat carried her kittens to the south, to the other side of the tracks.

In the late afternoon of October 12, 1918, on orders from the constable next door, Father and our neighbor, Esa (Ikola), went with him to fight the fire. When they arrived at another neighbor's place, a teenager hitched his newly broken colt to a stoneboat (a kind of sled used to carry things). On this they had a barrel which they filled from Hay Creek, and off they went on their errand. Reaching the top of a big hill they saw the miles and miles of countryside already in flames. Their barrel of water being of little use, they ran the colt back home. Father and Esa ran back to our place where Father quickly harnessed his horse to plow a firebreak around the buildings. He urged Esa to go home to protect his own place, but Esa was sure his farm was safe on the other side of the newly built Canadian Northern Railroad. The grade was gravel with no vegetation and would serve as a good firebreak, or so Esa figured. By the time Father had plowed two furrows the fire was upon him. With the gale wind the fire was in the air as much as on the ground, and soon the flaming debris ignited the grass and timber across the tracks. Esa exclaimed, "Vaivaanen!" and took off for home. His clothes snagged on the barbed wire fence, and his pants caught fire, but neither stopped him.

In the meantime, Mother milked the cows and turned them out. In the house my nine-year-old sister, Lillie, was urging my sister, Hilda, a seven-year-old, to carry in the wood as it was her "turn." "The fire will burn the house so it is no use to fill the woodbox," said Hilda. I was five at the time and it wasn't my "turn," so I didn't volunteer.

The woodbox unfilled, we were recruited to fight fire, so with gallon syrup pails we carried water on any sparks and flames within reach. Wild animals, rabbits, skunks, squirrels, etc. ran across the yard with no fear of us or the dog; their only enemy now was the raging fire! Mother drew water with rope and bucket from our winch-type well and carried it to Father who then carried it up the ladder to the roof of the house. The wooden shakes were tinder dry from weeks of drought, and the burning debris flying in the air was a constant threat. The neighbor's cows, wanting a drink, crowded around Mother's water pails making it doubly hard for her. When the fire neared the barn, Father took time out from carrying water up the ladder to get a colt from the barn. Sensing the danger outside the colt refused to go, so Father had to throw a gunny sack over its eyes and nose in order to lead him out. By then it was too late to rescue a young calf.

By late evening we three girls had exhausted ourselves so we were bedded down in a nearby plowed field. Wet quilts covered us but they dried out quickly in the intense heat so, every now and then, Mother threw water on them. Often six eyes peered from under the covers, once to see a wall of the log barn, the logs now bright red coals, tilt and fall to the ground. The pitiful cry of the calf was heard, but not for long. The six eyes also saw Father pull the burning wagon away from the haybarn. Later we were told how scared he was that the haybarn would burn, for in the root cellar underneath were one hundred pounds of dynamite and caps stored for future land clearing.

With pioneer stamina and Finnish "sisu," Father and Mother labored all night until five in the morning. Exhausted and suffering a migraine headache, Father lay down...Mother had good news, "Our cows and horses are safe by the hayshed in the west meadow." Miraculously, they were saved when all the meadow around was burned. Father could only say, "You must be dreaming!"

With ashes still caked on our faces from the long night, we counted our blessings—our family and home were safe, we had our cattle and two sheds full of hay. And, the dynamite was still intact!

Later my parents surveyed the fire losses and realized the many years of labor that went up in smoke that night. The barn, 7,500 feet of lumber, three haysheds, all the fences, farm implements and harnesses, and much more was lost. The all-important sauna was reduced to a pile of rock with metal pails warped beyond recognition. Ten cords of pine and birch firewood, split and ready for the stove, were gone. Not a stick was left to put in the unfilled woodbox!

Weeks later, in the totally burned out pasture, we found the hat

Father lost while plowing the firebreak. The hat wasn't even singed! The old mother cat came home with one kitten. Another was found in a neighbor's rock pile. She lost two other kittens, but Mother Cat couldn't tell us her story of that awful night. The rest of the fall and on into December we watched an "Old Faithful" of our own. From the snow-covered peat bog, columns of smoke and fire spewed out quite regularly, an eerie reminder of that night of flame.

Rural areas were hit hard by the fire.

Photo by Hugh McKenzie from the collection of CCHS

My Great Aunt

by Katie Caspersen

Excerpts from an article telling the story of Katie's great aunt. It was printed in the *Moose Lake Star Gazette*, October 10, 1991, p. 9, and reprinted in *The Fire Beast*.

It was a regular afternoon when panicking people ran into our small town of Moose Lake. These people said a large fire was coming this way but they didn't have any details. Nobody could contact us because the phone lines had burned down.

We began to worry about my father who was then a Lutheran minister at the Nordland Church, northwest of Denham, and other churches. He was gone at the time in a different town at a church.

Winds estimated at one hundred miles per hour, along with dry conditions, helped the fire along. We had to move fast. There was my mother, myself, Clemens, Norman, Juliet, Jeff, and Mildred. The children were ranging in age from thirteen to a newborn baby and my mother was pregnant.

There was nowhere to go and no time for preparation in a small town with only one thousand people. To make matters worse, dense smoke blocked the sun and made the afternoon look like the dark of night.

We could only take things we could carry. We put on our best Sunday clothes and took the family Bible and food. Our neighbor hurried us in his cart to the lake in the middle of our town.

As we arrived others were doing the same as us. We all dipped blankets in the lake and wrapped them around our bodies and over our heads so cinders and flying sparks could not hurt us. It made for a ghostly sight.

We walked into the lake as far as we could, holding the younger children about us. There was no panic. Remaining calm would save us.

It was the most frightening sight I've ever seen. The fire engulfed the town. We tried not to look but we couldn't help but watch our town disappear before us. While we watched, mother reached up to adjust the baby's blanket and a large cinder struck my mother in the forehead leaving an awful scar.

Along with us in the lake were farm animals. Some ran off in fear and were probably lost.

We were there for hours. We couldn't leave the lake because of the intense heat and dense smoke even after the fire passed. After a while we moved quietly back to our part of town. There were still smoldering embers strewn about like so many leaves in the fall.

What we saw when we got to what was once our home was unbelievable. The fire was so hot it literally petrified (turned to stone) wood fences, chairs, our sofa, and other items. Our personal belongings still sat there, but if they were touched they would disintegrate. We searched the house and found we had lost everything except for the food in our stone cellar. We returned to the lake, not yet knowing how many people had died.

We sat by the lake for two days because there was no transportation. Two days later a rescue party arrived and took us to a small town that hadn't been touched by the fire. Along the way we saw many farm and wild animals that had unsuccessfully tried to outrun the fire. From the small town we took a train to Duluth, which had escaped the fire.

We still hadn't heard from my father, but four days later he found us in Duluth. We met him with great joy, and while we had almost nothing, we had each other.

We stayed in Duluth with my aunt and later moved to North Dakota to begin anew. It was there that my mother delivered a healthy baby boy.

Even though this happened seventy-two years ago, the events, smells, colors, and sounds are forever burned in my memory.

National Guardsmen march in the ruined streets of Moose Lake.

Photo by Fred Levie from the collection of MLAHS

The Wedding

Excerpts from a CCHS manuscript by Beatrice Parks Gellerman.

This is a story with a happy ending. Written after the fire it tells us how people lived during the winter that followed the fire. Beatrice Parks and Lloyd Gellerman were married in Cloquet at her parents' fire shack on December 24, 1918.

    The day was the 23 of December, 1918, in Cloquet, Minnesota. The Armistice (the end of World War I) had been signed in November and Floyd was home on leave from the Navy. The Cloquet fire had burned the whole city (population 9,000) with the exception of Garfield School and a few outlying houses. We were living in a shack, 16 by 20 feet, heated by a wood stove, plus a little addition that contained a wood range, a wood box, and a few open shelves. We had just enough kettles, silver, and dishes for the five of us (Dad, Mother, Me, Lucile, and Merton, aged 2 1/2 years). We had one double bed, a couch that could sleep two, and a trundle bed for Merton which was stored in the daytime under the double bed. This sleeping area was enclosed by a rough board partition about 6 feet high with a curtain in the doorway.

    Floyd's mother and dad were living in Scanlon in a small temporary home. Floyd and I were engaged—I had my diamond that Floyd had bought for me at Tiffany's in New York when he was in port there. We had been spending as much time as possible together, but due to the lack of sleeping space in either home, we walked back and forth between the two homes. If we spent the day in Scanlon, Floyd would walk me home to Cloquet (3 miles) and then walk back to Scanlon to sleep or else spend the day in Cloquet and walk back to Scanlon. It was not what an engaged couple had in mind, after having been parted by the duration of the war. In Cloquet there wasn't even a movie where one could spend the evening.

    So on the afternoon of the 23rd of December, we were walking from Scanlon to Cloquet and Floyd said, "Why don't we just get married and go to Duluth on our honeymoon?" So we talked it over and decided to consult with Dad and Mother. Mother was plenty perturbed. She had had visions of a nice wedding the following summer in a new home that was already planned—after Floyd was out of the Navy.

109 Fire Storm: The Great Fires of 1918

However, Dad could see how we felt and said, "When would you like to do it?" Floyd said, "Tomorrow!" His leave was almost over.

So this plan was worked out. Our minister was living out at the University Forestry Station (situated 4 miles from Cloquet). Dad agreed to walk out there first thing in the morning to alert Reverend (William) Williams, there being no cars or telephones. Floyd was to walk to Scanlon to tell his folks and invite them to the wedding. Then he would take the train to Carlton where he would purchase a marriage license and a wedding ring, coming back on the next train in time to get married about 12 o'clock noon.

So we retired for the night, Floyd sleeping on the floor under the table with a minimum of bedding. The next morning early, we put the plans into motion. When Floyd's mother was told of our plans, she put her Christmas bread and rolls out in the breezeway to bake later, as they were having all of us for Christmas dinner the next day. Then they got ready—Milo was to be the best man and Dad Gellerman had to be alerted as he was at work as the Western Union operator in Cloquet.

At 910 Carlton Avenue things were really going in high gear. My mother and Lucile were cleaning the shack. Everything movable went out in the back yard in the snow so the rough board floor could be scrubbed. A new braided rug, that my Great Aunt Flo had sent us after the fire, was put in front of a homemade chest of drawers. The rest of the furniture was brought back in. I can't remember that I did much except to get dressed. I had two dresses—the one I had walked out in the night of the fire and a new very nice dark blue jersey dress which I had bought in Duluth. (The dress had) a round neckline and a front that had a design in soutache braid. The skirt had an overskirt or peplum as it was called. There wasn't much choice as to what I would wear. For jewelry, I wore a lavalier (a type of necklace) Floyd had given me and my diamond engagement ring. Floyd, of course, would be wearing his Navy dress uniform. One thing I remember clearly was the fresh fragrance of the shack. New, green, unfinished pine, a fresh scrubbed floor, and a cozy fire in the little heater. That memory remains with me still! Sixty-five years this Christmas!

Floyd arrived back from his errands about 11:45 a.m. Dad and the minister, Mr. Williams, got there about the same time. Mr. Williams was dressed in a plaid wool shirt, high topped boots, and jacket. Dad Gellerman, Mother Gellerman, Milo, and Doris arrived. My dad, mother,

Lucile, and Merton completed the guest list. Merton was all dressed up in a sailor suit and was cute as a button, sitting on a shelf that usually held the wash basin, and intensely interested in the whole proceedings.

The ceremony didn't take long—Milo was the best man, Lucile the bridesmaid. We stood on the rug in front of the chest. When it was over, Floyd slipped the minister a $5 bill. Mr. Williams filled out the marriage certificate and gave me the little book it was in. That evening when we looked at the book there was the $5 bill in an envelope with "Bea" written on the outside of it. A very simple inexpensive wedding.

Well, the next step was to get down to the depot (one mile away) to take the Great Northern train called "The Wooden Shoe" for Duluth. Floyd invited Milo and Lucile to accompany us to Duluth to have dinner with us. On the train Milo and Lucile had come prepared with a bag of rice and they proceeded to embarrass us and amuse the passengers by pouring rice down our necks. Floyd's sailor collar made a good funnel for that. The conductor came down the aisle and told Floyd "the monkey business would have to stop." Floyd politely told him we were all in favor of that. But it didn't stop, so when we reached the Union Station in Duluth, Floyd and I managed to give Milo and Lucile the slip and we ate our wedding dinner in the McKay Hotel by ourselves. Happily we hadn't told them where we planned to stay. To this day I don't know where they had dinner before going back to Scanlon and Cloquet on the evening train.

Christmas morning we had breakfast and then returned to Scanlon to spend Christmas day with the folks, returning to Duluth that evening. We spent several days in Duluth—getting our pictures taken and buying a new suit for me—a sort of plum colored wool with a seal skin collar and a new blouse to go with it.

When we returned to Cloquet we found our good friends and neighbors, Mr. and Mrs. Wight, had gone to Little Falls to spend Christmas with their parents and had told Dad and Mother "that Floyd and Bea could live in their shack for the rest of Floyd's leave." It was a cozy little shack being 12 by 16 feet over all in size. That was the size that was allotted when there were only two people in the family. Floyd had wired the Navy Department asking for an extension of his leave—for the reason "he had just gotten married." As the war was over, the extension was granted and so we had a few more days together before he left for the East via Niagara Falls on his honeymoon—all by himself—as he loved to tell in years to come.

Anna Dickie Olesen's Speech Before Congress

Excerpts from Anna Dickie Olesen's Speech Before Congress,
March, 1930

Anna Dickie Olesen was a politician and a well-known speaker on the Tent Chautauqua circuit. She was the wife of the superintendent of schools in Cloquet, Peter Olesen.

....Mr Davis said the other day that he stood here to support the right. I hope we are here to support the right; and not only the right but the courts of Minnesota...Now you may wonder why there are not more of us here who suffered through that fire. There are not so many of us here this afternoon. It costs money to come from Minnesota. It costs about $100, round trip, in railroad fare alone. Our people are with us in thought and mind...I heard the question asked yesterday why we signed our releases and signed away to the Government the right to the other that we lost, for which we received no money. I want to tell you that we signed under duress. It was a duress of poverty, the duress of broken hearts, the duress of broken homes. We had no more money to fight; and you, who know something of the psychology of disaster, know that we had fought as long as we could, having suffered what we did....I did not come here asking for sympathy, or that anybody else on our side comes here asking for any sympathy. We do not ask sympathy; we never have asked for sympathy. We only ask for justice—not sympathy in any way, shape or manner.

On the night of October 12, 1918, we were living in the city of Cloquet. Cloquet then was a city of about seven or eight thousand people...We did not think that there was any danger (from a forest fire); at least I never heard that anyone thought that there was danger; and the men went to work and the women were putting their children to bed (when the fire struck)...I want you to know that fire struck us at the worst possible time. It struck us in the fall, when we had our wood and our coal in. In our basement we had over $100 worth of coal; we had about $20 worth of wood; we all had our canned fruit: I would say there was in our cellar alone a hundred to one hundred and fifty dollars worth of fruit...that happened all over town. The people had winter supplies in, and that is why we suffered so much harder than if the fire had come in summer or in the spring.

The influenza was raging. We do not want to minimize that.

People were ill all over the country with influenza, although it had not reached its height then. The winter was coming on. Our boys were in the war —500 of them. So this fire struck us at the worst possible time.

(My husband) came rushing in and said... that the fire was coming across over the hills. I could not believe it. I could not think there was such a danger as that. I ran out of doors and took one look; and if you have ever seen a cyclone of fire, that is what I saw coming over the hills.

We hurried down to the (train) station. The wind was blowing 60 miles an hour...There was no wind that afternoon, but with that fire the wind came at 60 miles an hour. I had a hat when I started out, but I did not have it when I got to the train. The sand was cutting our faces.

Before we started my husband went out to warn an old lady that lived near us to leave, but she wouldn't go. After my husband got us on the train he went back after the old lady but she was gone. I thought surely she would have burned to death; but the next morning they found her in the sand pile in the park; she had gone to her daughter's grave and stayed there that night, and she had her two pet chickens in her hand when they found her in the morning and she was alive. There were no men on the train we got on. There were women and children, whites and Indians on this train. As we rushed to the train I was surprised at the calm of the people. There are two things that I remember about that fire as the train moved out. The people had taken their baby carriages to the railroad. There was a fence that runs along the railroad, and they had taken the baby carriages to the fence and taken the babies into their arms and to the train, and it was just one long line of baby carriages there along the fence. I think of that. Then I think of the other thing—the calm of our people; and the only words I heard that seemed to register on me were "Save the children!" I heard three men calling out "Save the children!" And we risked everything to get our children out. There were people there that night who never attempted to save a material thing but only sought to save the children. They left all material things to try to save the children, and they were heroic. The calm was marvelous...no amount of money the Government can ever pay us will compensate fully for those hours of anguish while we waited, fearing that our husbands and brothers and fathers would not come to us, and that they might have been destroyed in the city.

And I want to register this: that I never heard one person during that night of fire, or in the years of misery that followed, ever mur-

mur or complain about this loss. They just went to it to try to start their work again; and as those people passed that day, and we were passing out the clothes to them, already they were whispering among themselves, "It is said that the mills will start again."

And the hope of rebuilding the city lay upon the fact that the mills would start. A few mills had been spared by the fire. The paper mill had stood, and one other mill, as I remember it, and the box factory; and our people hoped that the mills would start again and give them work.

Only one school survived (The Garfield) and it was taken over by the Militia for a headquarters and the Red Cross for a hospital and our dead seemed to increase each day.

Finally the Militia left and the Red Cross operated at a different site. School was started. We lived in one of the cloakrooms, the three of us. The other school teachers lived in other cloakrooms similar to ours, and we ate in the basement on an old table that we had put together, of boards. And there we started to rebuild the schools. We lived there that winter. Meanwhile the people were living in shacks, here there, and everywhere, building up their little shacks, and suffering too; living, many of them in one room.

... To try to fix the liability for the fire we turned to our own lawyers, our local boys, to help us win justice. Two of them are here now—Mr. Frank Yetka and Mr. (Victor J.) Michaelson. I have known those boys when they were very much younger than they are today. I have seen them before any of them were lawyers. I have seen Mr. Frank Yetka struggling in night school trying to get an education, and Mr. Michaelson too. We turned to them and trusted them, and we never thought that we paid them too much for what they did for us in that fight.

Other lawyers were called in, and you know the story of the trials. I will not go into that. But we never felt that we had paid our lawyers too much.

Mr. Davis made the statement the other day, and I think the record will bear me out, that he paid out of his money; he used the term "my money." I have no right to take Mr. Davis' money. None of our people have. We have no right to take a cent of Government money unless the money is rightfully coming to us. The liability was fixed in our courts. Our courts of Minnesota said that my little home was burned 100 percent by the agents of the railroad administration. But when I came to get my money back, I get only half, although my

Fire Storm: The Great Fires of 1918 114

house was burned altogether, not half; they burned all my house, not half. They burned everything we had, not half of what we had, and we feel in right and justice and equity we should have that money back.

I want to say this one thing. Our settlers are Polish, Finnish, Austrian, and a good many of them Scandinavian. But the first three that I mention have come from governments that were oppressive. They fear government up there more than they do in a community that is all of American birth and ancestry. They were afraid of these government investigators. They were afraid of the government. They would have a tendency to respect courts, even more perhaps than people that were of a freer ancestry... I want you to know when they rallied together that night of the fire, October 12, to get out the settlers, they were using poor broken English the best they could, and I hate to see it laughed at, and I hate to see our courts laughed at. The people need the money very badly. Let us not blind justice and forget the poor because some with more money were partly reimbursed for their loss. The poor lost far more than others, and most of our people were of the poor class, just had enough to get along by laboring and struggling hard.

The faces of the fire sufferers tell the story.

Photo by International Film Service published in American Forestry, *November, 1918.*

On the steps of the family "fire shack," little Vivian Dobrowolski rocks the teddy bear that escaped the fire with her on the night of October 12, 1918.

Photo from the collection of Larry Luukkonen

REMEMBERING THE FIRES

In the years following the fires, efforts have been made to remember the fires and the fire sufferers by the erection of monuments, the writing of articles and books, and the recording of fire stories.

A monument was dedicated on October 12, 1929, in the Riverside Cemetery in Moose Lake, to "the Memory of Men, Women, and Children Who Perished in the Forest Fire of October 12, 1918." In Cloquet, a city park was named for Lawrence Fauley, the station agent credited with saving thousands of lives by lining up trains for the evacuation of the city. On the 50th anniversary of the fires on October 12, 1968, a monument in Fauley Park was dedicated to the fire survivors of Cloquet. On October 10, 1996, in downtown Kettle River, workers completed a monument with a brass plaque telling the history of the Kettle River fire area.

The inscription on the monument in Riverside Cemetery in Moose Lake is pictured in this photo.

Photo from the collection of MHS

The Moose Lake Area Historical Society has honored the fire survivors each year on the anniversary of the fires. The Society has collected many fire stories and taken a picture of the survivors every year. In 2003, MLAHS published a book called *1918 Fire Stories* and produced a play to commemorate the 85th anniversary of the fires. They have fire exhibits in the Depot and 1918 Fire Museum in the old Soo Line depot in Moose Lake.

This monument was dedicated on October 12, 1929, to those who perished in the fire. It can be seen in Riverside Cemetery in Moose Lake.

Photo from the collection of MHS

    The Carlton County Historical Society sponsored many activities for the 75th anniversary of the fires including the commissioning of a quilt embellished with fire photographs. For the 80th anniversary of the fires, CCHS invited artists and writers to submit work about the fires for an exhibition. Some of the fire stories collected at that time are included in this book. The Society has exhibits about the fires at the Carlton County History and Heritage Center in Cloquet. With the publication of *Fire Storm: The Great Fires of 1918*, CCHS adds to the growing body of written material about the fires.

    More information about the fires can be obtained by contacting the Carlton County Historical Society, 406 Cloquet Avenue, Cloquet, MN 55720, phone, 218/879-1938 or the Moose Lake Area Historical Society, 900 Folz Blvd., P. O. Box 235, Moose Lake, MN 55767, phone 218/485-4234 (seasonal).

Cloquet Mayor, Arlene Wolner, speaks at the dedication of the Cloquet fire monument in Fauley Park on October 12, 1968. Fire survivor, Paul Wagtskjold, is seated in the front right of the photo. Paul wrote his fire story and often visited classrooms to tell school children about the fires.

The inscription on the Cloquet monument is dedicated to those who came back and rebuilt Cloquet.

Photos from the collection of CCHS

Workers put the finishing touches on the "The 1918 Fire" monument in Kettle River on October 10, 1996.

Photo from the collection of CCHS

Survivors of the 1918 fire gathered in Moose Lake for this group photo in October, 1991.

Photo from the collection of CCHS

Fire Storm: The Great Fires of 1918 120

SUGGESTED READINGS

There have been numerous books, chapters of books, and articles written about the fires. Some of them are no longer in print and can be obtained only at libraries. The Carlton County Historical Society has a collection of fire materials that is available to interested researchers. This is a short list of some of the materials that can be purchased or borrowed from a library.

Carroll, Francis M. *Crossroads in Time: A History of Carlton County, Minnesota*. Carlton County Historical Society, Cloquet, 1987.

Carroll, Francis M. and Franklin R. Raiter. *The Fires of Autumn: the Cloquet-Moose Lake Disaster of 1918*. Minnesota Historical Society Press, St. Paul, 1990.

Carroll, Francis M. and Marlene Wisuri. *Reflections of Our Past: A Pictorial History of Carlton County, Minnesota*. Donning Company, Virginia Beach, VA, 1997.

Fahlstrom, Paul. *Anna Dickie and Peter Oleson: Notable Citizens of Cloquet*. Carlton County Historical Society, Cloquet, 1996.

The Fury of the Flames: A Pictorial History of the Great Forest Fires of Northern Minnesota, October 12-15, 1918. Carlton County Historical Society, Cloquet; Moose Lake Historical Society, Moose Lake, 1998.

Manni, Edwin E. *History and Stories: Kettle River, Automba, Kalevala, and Surrounding Area*. Self published, 1978.

1918 Fire Stories. Moose Lake Area Historical Society, Moose Lake, 2003.

Peacock, Thomas D. *A Forever Story: The People and Community of the Fond du Lac Reservation*. Fond du Lac Band of Lake Superior Chippewa, Cloquet, 1998.

Piippo-Lambert, Carol Illikainen. *Firebeast: the Fires of 1918*. Moose Lake Area Historical Society, Moose Lake, 1994.

Reed, Daniel, *Automba: A Study of a Finnish Timber Boomtown*. Automba Publishing. Kettle River, MN, 1990.

www.cpinternet.com/~kjackson/fire.html

"Looking Through the Attic Window," is a wall quilt commemorating 75th anniversary of the Great Fires of 1918. It was designed and quilted in 1993 by the Pine Needle Quilters of Carlton. It features cyanotype prints of photos from the CCHS collection.

NEWSPAPER HEADLINES

Although the newspaper headlines and articles from the time of the fire were not always totally accurate, they offer an overview of fire incidents and can provide valuable insight into fire history.

NORTHEAST MINNESOTA SWEPT BY FLAMES; MANY TOWNS GONE

Over 400 Burned to Death in Moose Lake District Alone—All Homes in Cloquet Leveled—Home Guards Organize Relief Work——Bodies Strew Roadsides.

HUNDREDS KETTLE RIVER FARMERS LOSE FAMILIES, BUILDINGS, STOCK

Farmers' Dispatch, *October 15, 1918*

28 Villages Wiped Off Map; Fire Toll Steadily Increases

Work of Bringing in Bodies Barely Begun as Toll Mounts Higher and Higher---Many Towns Now Safe --Dead Found in Piles

The Duluth News Tribune, *October 15, 1918*

CLOQUET, CITY OF PINES, DESTROYED TO LAST BUILDING

Mass of Ruins, With Only Paper Mills Left Standing at Outskirts to Mark Place.

The Duluth News Tribune, *October 14, 1918*

MOOSE LAKE ONE SAD RUIN

Dazed, Stupefied Groups Look Unmoved on Heaps of Corpses; Relief Crews Labor

The Duluth News Tribune, *October 15, 1918*

SPREAD OF NEW FIRES IS CHECKED BY THE MILITARY

The Duluth Herald
October 16, 1918

FEDERAL LAND BANK COMES TO AID OF STRICKEN FARMERS

Will Do All Possible Towards Rebuilding Devastated Section.

To Encourage Farmers to Rebuild Homes and Continue Farming.

every assistance within their power to those unfortunate farmers and their families as well as all others affected in the burned-over regions in Northern Minnesota and Wisconsin. This calamity which has come upon them so suddenly has virtually destroyed thousands of homes. The loss of life can not be estimated in a material sense though the loss of property can. Every means possible should be taken towards restoring to those unfortunates as much as possible that which they previously had.

"The Federal Land Bank of St. Paul purposes to do everything in its power towards assisting in rebuilding this devastated section. In the affected area there are between twelve and fif-

The Duluth Herald, October 16, 1918

ARMS OF DULUTH OPEN TO VICTIMS; FIRST AID GIVEN

Armory Thronged With Patients Cared For by Red Cross Women—Heroic Rescues.

The Duluth News Tribune October 13, 1918

"GREATER CLOQUET" IS TO BE SLOGAN

Postoffice Opened on Island and Plans for Rebuilding Going Ahead.

Cloquet, Minn., Oct. 16.—(Special to The Herald.)—Cleaning up after the fire that wiped out this city started yesterday. Postmaster E. S. Schiebe has opened a temporary postoffice on the island, where few buildings were burned, and is now receiving and sending out mail. Mr. Schiebe wishes to inform all Cloquet people now in Superior and Duluth that their mail will be forwarded to them if they will furnish him with their temporary address; otherwise it will be held here. A telephone connection with the outside world has also been established on the island.

The Duluth Herald, October 16, 1918

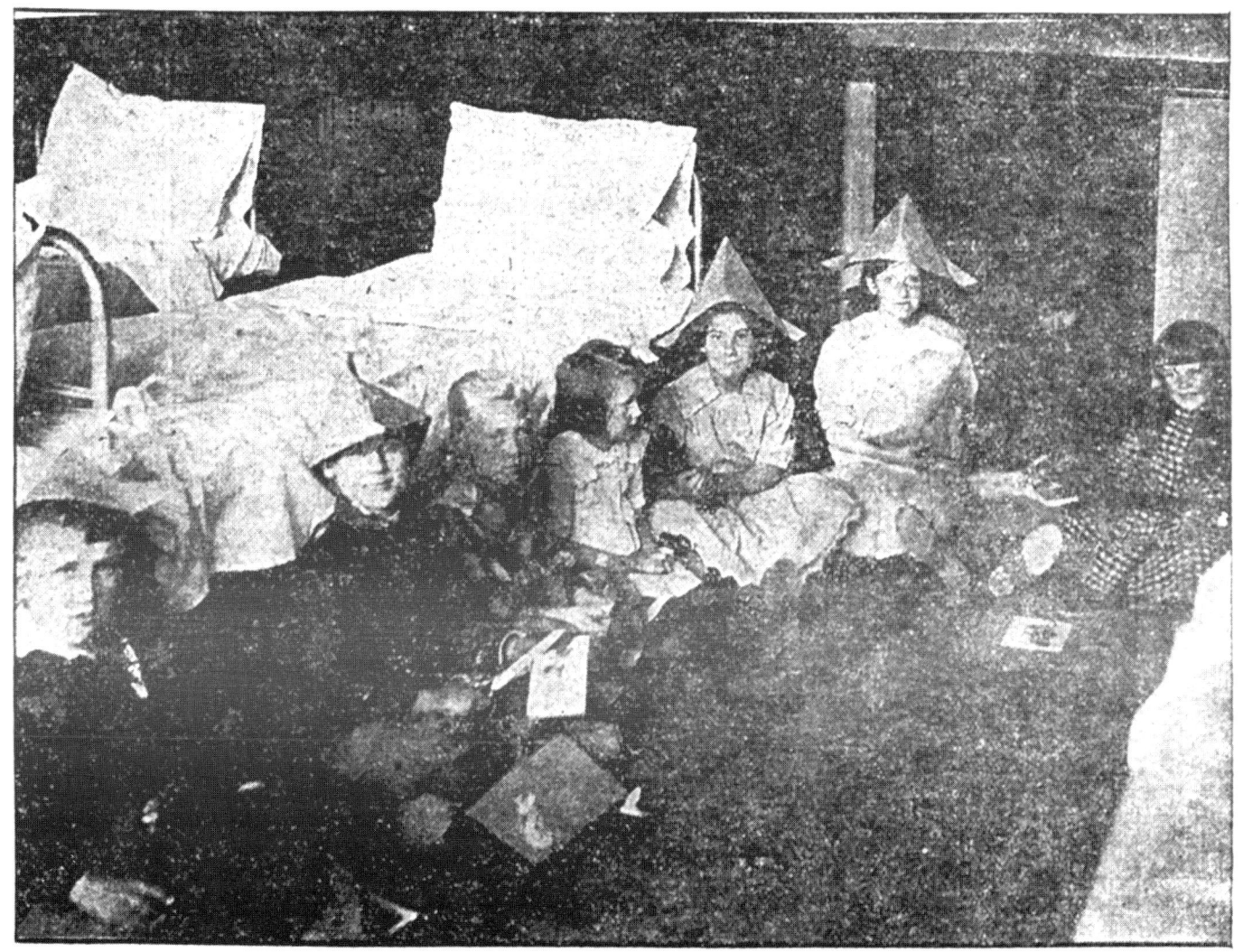

The Duluth News Tribune, *October 18, 1918*

ABOUT THE AUTHORS

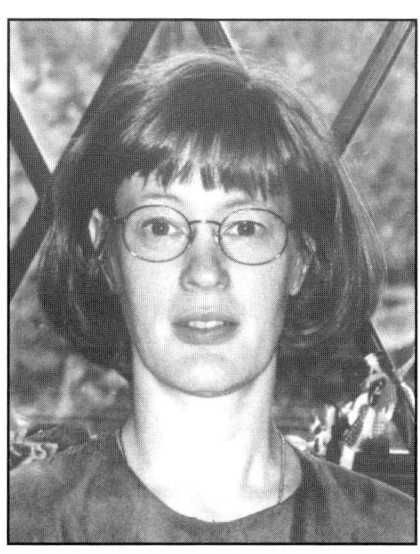

Christine Skalko has served as a reference librarian at the University of Wisconsin Superior and the College of St. Scholastica. Recently she has served as educator and archivist for the Carlton County Historical Society and archivist for the Diocese of Duluth. She holds a Master's degree in Library Science from the University of Minnesota Minneapolis.

Marlene Wisuri is the Director of the Carlton County Historical Society. She has co-authored several books including *The Good Path*, an Ojibwe learning and activity book for kids. She has taught photography at several colleges and universities and her photographic work has been widely exhibited. She has a Master of Fine Arts degree from the University of Massachusetts-Dartmouth.

Photo by Kathryn Nordstrom, Studio One